Enough
Is
Enough

Enough *Is* Enough

GRACE FOR THE RESTLESS HEART

John F. Westfall

HarperSanFrancisco
Zondervan Publishing House
Divisions of HarperCollins*Publishers*

Credits for reprinted material continue on page 166.

FIRST EDITION

LC 91–58990
ISBN 0–06–069289–8

93 94 95 96 97 ❖ RRD(H) 10 9 8 7 6 5 4 3 2 1

This edition is printed on acid-free paper that meets the American
National Standards Institute Z39.48 Standard.

This book is dedicated with love to my parents, Frank and Laurel Westfall, and to my brothers and sister, Richard, Karl, and Florence. Each brings something unique to the family table, and I'm sure we all remember different things about our life together, but through it all is the unmistakable thread of grace.

CONTENTS

ACKNOWLEDGMENTS

There are many people in my life who have extended grace to me. They have each demonstrated that we don't always get what we deserve but much, much more.

Bruce Larson called me by a new name and set me free from old attitudes so that I could live with freedom and grace.

Tom Burley is a faithful friend who stays closer than a brother.

Marianne Peirsol, Darrel Young, Sandy Gwinn, Jerry O'Leary, and Rich Hurst were true partners in ministry who brought encouragement and accountability (not to mention that amazing chocolate-cola cake).

Special thanks to Joanne Meads, my administrative assistant, who fills the office with joy and helps me stay focused on what is most important at any given moment.

Randy Rowland is more than a co-host for our Everyday People radio program. He also is a great friend, commiserator, dreamer, and all-round wild and fun guy who totally understands my dependence on classic rock and roll. (Is there any other kind?)

I'm grateful for the loving support of my new family at the Walnut Creek Presbyterian Church, where I serve as Senior Pastor. Together we are discovering the adventure of following Christ into a bright and hopeful future.

Of course, most of all I'm grateful for the love and support of my wife, Eileen, and my son, Damian. They have weathered some pretty fierce storms with me and seem to love me anyway. . . . It must be grace.

INTRODUCTION

Not long ago, while checking in with a small group of friends, I found myself struggling to explain exactly how I was feeling. In spite of doing well outwardly, I seemed to be frustrated and unhappy deep inside. In the course of sharing I began stringing together a typical list of run-of-the-mill struggles, problems, and various disappointments that I was coping with at the time. "When I get through all of these things," I told them, "maybe then I will be happy."

Most of my friends were used to hearing me share like this and were unfazed. One man in the group kept playing analyst by probing into the different parts of my life to see where the problems were coming from. "I just want to know why you aren't satisfied," he said. (Don't you just hate it when you share vulnerably and others jump in trying to fix you?)

As we talked, we were all a little surprised to see just how marvelous my life really is. I am married to a wonderful, beautiful woman, who for no apparent reason still finds me challenging and charming. Though not without our share of tensions and problems, we aren't like the man who said, "My wife and I were blissfully happy for twenty years, and then we met." Our son is a gift from God; he is smarter, more confident, and more verbal than I will ever be.

I love my job. It is challenging, creative, and there are times when I can't believe I'm actually paid to work here. My spiritual life seems to be strong and constantly deepening. I am still on speaking terms with the Lord, and I'm growing in my ability to trust him on a daily basis.

Physically, I am pretty healthy. The car starts most of the time, the house is still standing, and our dog is still glad to see me when I come home. Even my golf game is improving. Who could ask for anything more? Not a bad life. . . .

So why wasn't I satisfied? What was wrong with me that I should feel a gnawing discontent when I was living a pretty good life by most standards?

Finally, I looked up at my friends and said, "I know God is smiling on me right now. . . . I feel his love, and I realize how blessed I am. But I can't help feeling it just isn't enough." That evening, I determined to find out what's gone wrong.

What has gone wrong? If we are to discover the answers, it is important to know what the problems are. Perhaps if we go back to the beginning and see what happened in the biblical account of the creation and fall, we will find clues to the dilemmas that so often leave us restless and dissatisfied today.

Sometimes I'm asked if I really believe in the biblical story of creation as it is presented in the opening chapters of Genesis. While I may not be able to present adequate scientific evidence for the creation account of Scripture, I am convinced that I, along with many other people, can attest to the fact that what happened so long ago occurs repeatedly in our everyday lives.

Just like it was "In the Beginning . . . " (Gen. 1:1–3), so we find it today. God's spirit moves over the vague and undefined terrain of our lives, allowing our world to take shape in a meaningful way. All of our attempts to order, shape, fill, and schedule our world can't hide the fact that life apart from God's creative work is without form and void. Apart from God's creative presence, our lives are empty and pointless. That is the way it was back then and that is the way it is now.

As Christians we soon discover that without Christ to light our way, we feel powerless to live purposely or effectively. We may by our best efforts strike an occasional match and see a glimpse of what could be for an instant, but inevitably the darkness enfolds us and we are left alone in the dark. We often try our best to pretend that we aren't afraid, all the while knowing that we are powerless to push back the darkness.

Suddenly, God's word rings out through the darkness. It rumbles over the hills, chimes in our ears, and resonates in our quaking hearts, "Let there be light." And there is light.

In that moment when God's word is heard, the darkness vanishes and we see the truth for the first time: The darkness cannot harm us; the isolation and loneliness was an illusion; our lives are not meaningless; our world is not without form.

We see the truth about ourselves: our shortcomings, our rebellion, our fears, and our failures. We also see that in spite of these things we are loved and valued as the creation of God, made in his image, to be in fellowship with him. We are equipped and empowered to overcome every obstacle as we live out our relationship with the living God. We know without any doubt that God is smiling on us. We are the ones he loves.

I think it would be great if the story ended there. I love big, happy endings when everyone is content and they live happily ever after. Isn't it too bad that the Bible is not a collection of fairy tales? But the Bible has too much reality to be mere story-book stuff. It's always prodding us to deal with real life.

There was trouble in paradise! Genesis 3:1–7 provides an account of the encounter between Eve and the tempter. First we find confusion over what God has spoken; then there is misunderstanding about God's word. Then a lie, in direct opposition to God's word. Finally, the desire to be more, have more, know more . . . all resulting in sin, which is compounded by covering up, hiding, fear, and blame. In that moment the darkness begins to return to the land.

Eve and Adam seemed to have everything. A great relationship, all of their physical and emotional needs met. They had meaningful, purposeful lives. They had an intimate, personal relationship with God. There was nothing they lacked to live and prosper in a perfect world.

In fact, the only thing that was lacking was the knowledge of evil. In their grasping for this knowledge, in their desire to be like God, they gained what they were missing: Now they understood through personal experience the pain of deception, sin, guilt, disobedience, shame, broken relationships, blaming others, and ultimately death. They got all the things they thought they wanted—and lost the good thing they had.

Have you ever wondered why we have to suffer for Adam and Eve's mistake? Just as I begin to get a little smug, I realize that I am no more satisfied with my life than they were with theirs. Isn't it amazing that no matter how much we have or how much we accomplish, we never seem to be totally satisfied?

The fact is that we are not content to be merely people in relationship *with* God. We want to *be* God, recreating the world in our own image. Modern-day philosopher Erma Bombeck once said, "God created man, but I could have done much better." We want to design our surroundings, control the people in our lives, and manipulate our circumstances. We want to be God.

This desire lies at the very root of our dissatisfaction and restless hearts. Satisfaction and fulfillment can never be linked to achievement or circumstances. For there will always be something missing deep inside. Oscar Levant realized this when he said, "It's not what you are, it's what you don't become that hurts."

Unfortunately, most of us spend our time and energy striving to be more, do more, achieve more, and become more. But we usually don't realize that these efforts are doomed to fail, often leaving us bitter, disappointed, and frustrated. The only way we will ever be fully satisfied is to accept God's provision or antidote for our sin—his gift of grace.

The Gospel writer in John 1:14 reminds us, "And the Word became flesh and dwelt among us, full of grace and truth." Grace is the missing ingredient that releases us from achievement-oriented living. It is the power to forgive and begin anew. It is the empowering gift that allows us to live beyond our limitations. It is the unconditional acceptance that says, "You are home where you belong."

I don't know why, but it seems that grace is one of the most talked about and the least experienced ingredients in our lives. I have spent years teaching, preaching, and writing about grace. I cajole and even occasionally harangue people to accept God's grace for them. But when it comes to my own life, I find myself going to great lengths to avoid experiencing grace. I don't particularly like feeling out of control. Maybe that is why I tend to avoid situations in which the free gift of grace is needed. All of us are in some ways fugitives of grace. I know the ache of ambivalence. How often do we find ourselves fleeing from and longing for the same thing?

The easy answer is painfully obvious. I know that I need to finally stop running and accept the gift. I also know that it doesn't matter whether we are at the beginning point of our spiritual journey, perhaps considering whether or not to accept

Christ into our lives for the first time, or if we are like the woman who admitted that though she was a Christian for thirty-five years, she never really knew that God loved her. Whoever we are, wherever we are, there is grace for us.

John 1:16 reminds us that "from his fullness have we all received, grace upon grace." The Greek word *anti* has been translated to mean "upon." It is often translated to mean "over and against." The implication is that if we look beyond grace we will find still more. If we flee opposite grace, or go in a direction opposing grace, we will still find grace waiting for us. In other words, "From his fullness he has given us all grace *against* grace."

Yet in the face of this overpowering love I remain strangely and relentlessly dissatisfied. How can I get to the point where I can accept this radical grace for myself? It's easier to tell others about their need for grace than it is for me to allow grace into my own life. This book is personal because grace itself is dramatically personal. I invite you to come with me on this restless journey as we look at our lives and discover hidden treasures among the usual collection of hopes and fears.

PART I

Grace to Overcome

CHAPTER ONE

Overcoming Insecurity

Everything must degenerate into work if anything
is to happen.
PETER DRUCKER
author of *The Effective Executive*

*W*HEN it comes to insecurity, I'm reminded of the words
of the king in *The King and I* who in frustration declared, "It's a
puzzlement!" We too have conflicting thoughts and emotions
that are very puzzling to us. It's puzzling to me that I feel insecure so much of the time when friends tell me I have the outward
appearance of confidence and achievement. Learning to overcome the insecurity that wells up at unexpected moments may be
one of the most needed and most difficult things we can do.

Three Myths About Life

The roots of insecurity are planted deep within us. The ways in
which we look at life can either free us to overcome insecurity or
cause insecurity to overcome us. Our beliefs about ourselves,
about other people, even about life itself influence us in powerful
ways. In order to overcome insecurity, it is helpful to recognize

some of the myths about life that may block our efforts to overcome insecurity.

God's will is always easy.   Phil had been out of college for a
few years and needed to make a decision about his job. Sitting in
my office, he shared about his struggles at work. "I'm confused,"
he said. "I prayed that God would lead me to the right job, and
at first everything was great. But lately there have been so many
problems and hassles, I wonder if this was ever what God intended for me." I knew how he felt. Many times I've wanted to
quit or give up on a job, a relationship, or a church just because it
was not easy. Sometimes I believe this myth.

We can become discouraged when we mistakenly assume that
if we follow Christ there will be no obstacles, disappointments, or
setbacks on our journey of faith. It is amazing that this myth is so
widely held when there is no apparent reason to believe it. The
Bible is filled with realistic warnings of difficult and often painful
experiences, particularly if we follow God's will. Well-intentioned
friends have warned me that if I have a difficult time I need to
evaluate whether I am following God's will. We sometimes see
struggle, setback, sickness, and even hard work as clues that we
are "out of God's will." Unfortunately, the Christian life is still
real life, and life is not the absence of obstacles but a continual
process of moving over, around, and through them. Psychiatrist
Scott Peck began *The Road Less Traveled* with the important reminder: "Life is difficult." When I first read these words, a wave of
relief swept over me. The myth of the easy life began to crumble,
and I knew an authentic life was about to emerge. Along the way
I find that following God's plan will eventually require work.

We should always feel confident.   Some people feel insecure
and then feel guilty about feeling insecure, which only leaves
them feeling more insecure. Feelings are not rational; therefore it
does not help to reason by telling yourself or others to stop feel-

ing insecure. They may understand all of your reasons and agree intellectually, but the feeling will remain gnawing away in the inner recesses of their minds.

The mysterious power of the gospel is such that we can live courageously in the face of an uncertain future, whether we feel confident or not. Regardless of the difficulties we face, there is a strength that helps us live with courage.

I heard about a young high school student, Jason Martin, who as a teenager discovered how to live courageously even when seriously ill. When doctors diagnosed a brain tumor in Jason, no one would have blamed him if he just gave up and lamented the unfairness of life. Instead, while undergoing intensive treatment for the diagnosed brain tumor, Jason got to work and completed his goal of earning his Eagle Scout badge by assembling a comprehensive directory of organizations and agencies that serve the needy in his hometown of Seattle.

"Many people would have put such a demanding chore aside, but not Jason," his mother said. "He just kept going as if nothing was the matter. He wouldn't let anything get him down. He's been calm even after the surgery when we learned the tumor was malignant."

At the ceremony where Jason was awarded his Eagle badge, one speaker commented that "Jason is the kind of person that if you gave him a basket of rotten apples, he'd still find a way to make an apple pie."

What you see is what you get. Sometimes we get fooled by appearances. It is easy to make conclusions and judgements based on appearances and first impressions. When our personal insecurities align with surface expectations, we may be sent into a spiral and think we have no chance, or we may act braver than we actually are.

The line between courage and fear is very thin. I love to hear about bold and daring action in the face of unsettling danger.

But not all apparently bold action stems from courage. At a conference recently author Charles Garfield related the following story of mistaken courage.

> A very wealthy man bought a huge ranch in Arizona, and he invited some of his closest associates in to see it. After touring some of the 1500 acres of mountains and rivers and grasslands, he took everybody to the house. The house was as spectacular as the scenery, and out back was the largest swimming pool you have ever seen. However, this gigantic swimming pool was filled with alligators.
>
> The rich owner explained this way: "I value courage more than anything else. Courage is what made me a billionaire. In fact, I think that courage is such a powerful virtue that if anybody is courageous enough to jump into that pool, swim through those alligators and make it to the other side, I'll give them anything they want, anything—my houses, my land, my money." Of course, everybody laughed at the absurd challenge and proceeded to follow the owner into the house for lunch . . . when they suddenly heard a splash. Turning around, they saw this guy swimming for his life across the pool, thrashing at the water, as the alligators swarmed after him.
>
> After several death-defying seconds, the man made it unharmed to the other side. The rich host was absolutely amazed, but he stuck to his promise. He said, "You are indeed a man of courage, and I will stick to my word. What do you want? You can have anything—my house, my land, my money—just tell me what you want and it is yours." The swimmer, breathing heavily, looked up at the host and said, "I just want to know one thing—who pushed me in that pool?"

Things are not always the way they appear. Usually it is when we look below the surface that we come to understand the real issues, the strengths and weaknesses, and the real battles that are going on. When we get beyond the myths and presuppositions about life, we can see God's strategy for overcoming insecurity.

The Old Testament book of Numbers shows us a glimpse of the struggle the Israelites had in their effort to overcome insecurity. It can be helpful to learn from their experience when we feel insecure and over our heads with the obstacles of life. There were three steps to their downfall: They compared, became frightened, and finally despaired.

Like many of us in this modern world, the Israelites believed in market research. Before they made a leadership decision, they decided to do some assessments to help them decide whether or not to enter the land God had given them. Initially they heard reports from the returning spies and began to compare themselves with the inhabitants of the land. "The land through which we have gone, to spy it out, is a land that devours its inhabitants, and all the people that we saw in it are men of great stature. . . . And we seemed to ourselves like grasshoppers, and so we seemed to them" (Num. 13:32, 33).

Too often we compare ourselves with others. When we do this we usually lose. There is always someone who is better than we are and someone who is worse. No matter who we are or how far we've come, we are either looking up or looking down at someone. Building our self-esteem by comparing ourselves with others will never enable us to overcome insecurity. It is a one-way street to disappointment. Comparison robs us (whether we are the comparer or the comparee) of the dignity that is our rightful inheritance as a unique, one-of-a-kind individual who is created and loved by God.

No one else in the world will ever be exactly like you. Your experiences, victories, defeats, abilities, limitations, hopes, and fears make you special. When we forget this and line ourselves up against others, we lose. There is no way to categorize ourselves and make the comparison valid. We end up like Yogi Berra, who on the first day of spring training ordered the players to "line up over there alphabetically according to height." We become confused by our comparisons, and we do not know which basis to use for our decisions.

After God's people compared themselves with the inhabitants of the land, they were overcome by fear. "Then all the congregation raised a loud cry; and the people wept that night" (Num. 14:1). What happened to the Israelites can be a common experience for us today when we become overwhelmed with insecurity and fear as a result of comparing ourselves with others. Sometimes our insecurities and fears do not surface when we are awake and alert, but tend to fill our mind in the night when we are trying to sleep.

I meet regularly with a group of friends for Bible study and personal sharing. One evening we sat around a table checking in as we do each week. Coincidentally, each person mentioned that he or she had woken up at about 3:30 A.M. the night before. Anxieties, fears, apprehensions, anger, and a variety of emotions had conspired to rob us of our sleep.

When it became obvious that most of us were up at the same time, we began to laugh and finally agreed that in the future we may need a signaling system whereby we could alert the others in the small group that we were up and available to accept visitors in the middle of the night.

What wakes you in the middle of the night? What makes your hands clammy and starts your heart beating faster? These "sleep robbers" play on our insecurity to wear us down and leave us tired, scared, and emotionally drained.

Like us, the people of Israel were tired and scared. They came so far. They endured hardship, burdens, and crises. They worked hard and trusted God to bring them to this land. Now at the threshold of their dream, they discovered new obstacles that scared them more than anything they had to endure before.

Perhaps their fear was less concerned with giants in the land and more concerned with the fact that they were uncertain that they could be strong, creative, brave, smart, or big enough to handle the new challenges before them. And their insecurities grew as they wailed and wept the night away.

"And all the people of Israel murmured against Moses and Aaron; the whole congregation said to them, 'Would that we had died in the land of Egypt! Or would that we had died in this wilderness! Why does the Lord bring us into this land, to fall by the sword? Our wives and our little ones will become a prey; would it not be better for us to go back to Egypt? And they said to one another, 'Let us choose a captain and go back to Egypt'" (Num. 14:2–3).

God's people immediately began to despair, blaming Moses and Aaron for their predicament. "It's their fault! We wouldn't be in this mess if it weren't for their questionable leadership." Despair sets in when all hope is gone. Fear turns to anger and bitterness; then it dissolves into irrational responses.

This points out what some psychologists have been telling us for a long time. It is often more comfortable to stay in the mess that we are familiar with than to step out and face a potential mess that is new and different. We understand that. New situations are somehow more difficult to face than our old, familiar pain.

Breaking the Cycle of Insecurity

If we want to rise above the shackles of insecurity, we need a fresh power and a new perspective of ourselves and our world. It is not easy to overcome a lifetime of insecurity, but it is very possible to change. When we finally get to the place where we are ready to let go of some of our insecure feelings, we need to find some tangible steps to help us move beyond those feelings. The apostle Paul writing in 2 Timothy provides some handles to help us overcome our feelings of insecurity.

Reminder of love. If love is the antidote to fear ("Perfect love casts out fear"), then Timothy gets a special dose from Paul who reminds him that he is loved. "To Timothy, my *beloved* child: Grace, mercy and peace" (2 Tim. 1:2, italics mine). In fact, the first five verses of this letter are a litany of encouragements, memories, and affirmations, as well as a general outpouring of love. When I know I am loved, it is easier to overcome my insecurities. There is freedom to struggle, to succeed, even to fail because I'm loved.

When we read these verses it is easy to jump to the mistaken conclusion that if we had someone like Paul in our lives to love and encourage us, we would not be insecure either. But to overcome our insecurity, we need to express love in tangible ways to others. We do not need to receive more love; we need to give more love. We must be aggressive in our bestowal of grace to those in our lives.

We should each have a list of people in our lives that we affirm and nurture. We pray for them and call out affirmations for them. We encourage them in their faith and remind them that they are special. In effect, we become "Pauls" to them.

Giving love in this way will have a remarkable effect on our attitude. We will no longer compare, fear, or despair. In fact, we will have no time to struggle with insecurity because we will be cheerleading for someone else. In the process we will become involved in the most important ministry any person could possibly undertake: the nurturing and upbuilding of a fellow Christian.

Rekindle the flame. The second step to overcome insecurity is to rekindle, or as another translation says, "fan into flame the gift of God, which is in you" (2 Tim. 1:6, NIV).

The Greek word *charis* that is translated "gift," or "spiritual gift," literally means "grace." God has graced or gifted every Christian with special and unique abilities to minister and build up the Body. Too often we allow these gifts to lie dormant or undeveloped through lack of use.

I talk with people all the time who feel they are not gifted. The truth is that most of us feel that way. So when we think about having special gifts from God, it doesn't ring true for us. In fact, most of the people I know feel that they have little, if anything, to offer in ministry.

It is easy to lose sight of the fact that God made us and loves each of us as a one-of-a-kind miracle. It is exciting to realize our lives can be full, rich, and individual because God has given us the gift of marvelous diversity. It is time to "fan in to flame the gift of God that is in us." In so doing we move out in effective ministry, overcoming insecurity along the way.

Resist the timid trap. Have you ever considered that being timid is a sin? Sin is missing the mark of God's intention for our lives. When we fall into the trap of acting timid, we miss the mark of God's best for us. "God did not give us a spirit of timidity," writes Paul, "but a spirit of power, and love, and self-control" (2 Tim. 1:7). I am coming to believe that when we act timid we are in effect refusing to allow the Holy Spirit free expression in our lives.

Our ability is not in our self-confidence or personal ability. Rather it lies in Jesus Christ and his power at work in us. Paul writes, "But I am not ashamed, for I know whom I have believed, and I am sure that he is able to guard until that Day what has been entrusted to me" (2 Tim. 1:12). Knowing that we are secure in Christ and that he is able to meet every need, obstacle, and insecurity we may encounter gives us strength to live with confidence.

CHAPTER TWO

Overcoming Obsession

My whole life is dedicated to my desperate need for stardom, attention, and applause.
JACKIE MASON

"*I*'M not obsessive," insists a friend of mine. "I just pursue things with laser-beam clarity and single-mindedness." Perhaps one word that may come to symbolize this decade of the nineties is *obsession*. We may become marked and eventually be held prisoner by our obsessions.

It's no secret that we are driven people. The drive to acquire and prosper can push us forward to pursue things or money, or symbols of success and wealth. While there is nothing inherently wrong with motivation to move forward, some of us become single-minded in the pursuit of goals or dreams to the exclusion of other things. As we pursue the object of our desire, it soon fills our time and energy and becomes the sole focus of our attention.

Advertising agencies understand this and present images to feed our current obsessions. One series of ads that appears in popular magazines promotes a cologne called Obsession for Men. The ads are provocative and intriguing, and they tell us something about ourselves and our attitudes toward each other and life.

The first Obsession ads showed a tangled web of nude bodies interwoven together so figures are indistinguishable from each other. Arms, legs, and torsos are twisted together in such a way that it is indiscernible who is who. One cannot tell which are men and which are women, or which leg belongs with which arm or foot. The text simply says, "Obsession for Men."

The message is clear. Our dream is to be lost in an impersonal, faceless mass of sensuality. We don't want to be known or seen for the whole person we are. We prefer to lose ourselves in a swirl of impersonal, nonrelational sexuality. This is man's obsession. The popularity of the promotions may indicate that this is women's obsession as well.

Then, as changing roles and identities brought confusion and blurring of expectations, a new ad appeared. This time a solitary muscular man stands with a beautiful nude woman slung over his shoulder like a sack of potatoes, again with the words, "Obsession for Men." The message is clear: Alan Alda is dead! No more weak Mr. Nice Guy. Enough of the sensitive-but-wimpy American male. Bring back the strong-yet-supportive American who can carry not only the weight of the world on his shoulders but also the weight of a woman who has obviously graduated from a weight-loss clinic. Now this is an obsession we can sink our teeth into!

We have grown up a little now, and times are changing. In a recent magazine I saw a soft, warm picture of a tough-yet-tender man lying on a bed holding a tiny, fragile newborn baby on his manly chest. The words on the page say it all: "Obsession for Men." Images of family, commitment, caring, vulnerability, nurture, and hope for the future all come to mind.

There are many different kinds of obsessions. We obsess over people, relationships, children, family members, even movie stars or sports figures. We even use food, cars, homes, or power tools as objects of obsession. We can obsess over anything that we desire or fear. We obsess over disappointments and failures. Worry and anxiety can grow into a form of obsession.

I think it is safe to say that most of us find ourselves obsessing at times in our lives. We also know that it does no good to try to stop thinking about things over which we obsess. Try to not think of pink elephants for five minutes. Of course pink elephants immediately fill your awareness. It isn't enough to just stop thinking about things over which we obsess. It is more helpful to look at our thoughts as signals that can alert us to unacknowledged needs and fears that lie beneath the surface of our conscious minds. These needs and fears have a way of coming out in one form or another, often upsetting our apparently tranquil life.

It is possible to confuse our needs and fears so that we are unsure of our feelings and motivations. In the movie *Moonstruck,* a mother was having a talk in a restaurant with a handsome college professor. Suddenly she asked him, "Why do men run around and cheat on their wives?" He responded predictably that they wanted to feel love and excitement or perhaps they were unhappy at home. Then she interrupted him, saying, "I think it is because they are afraid to die." "Yes," he answered, "that is why they cheat."

I love this poignant scene because it reminds me that my rash and often destructive behavior can be a signal that there are unresolved fears lurking beneath the surface of my tranquil life. If they are ignored or left unattended, they may eventually surface in surprising and hurtful ways.

What begins innocently enough in the back of my mind soon looms in the forefront of thoughts, dominating my vision and draining my energy and creativity. Sometimes we have "magnificent obsessions" in which we long for the pleasure and good feeling that comes with the thoughts. Other times we are haunted by fierce and foreboding obsessions that torment and wear us down.

Whatever form our obsessions take, they have one thing in common: If unbridled, they will undermine our freedom and stifle our growth. We will eventually enslave ourselves to the things we cling to in our minds.

When we embrace a goal, idea, or vision of the way things should be, we become like a heat-seeking missile. Nothing can distract us or veer us away from our single-minded quest. This can be particularly unsettling when it happens in our spiritual lives.

Looking at the Gospels, it is apparent that the early disciples had clear ideas about Jesus and his ministry. They undoubtedly expected him to establish a political kingdom (with them in positions of power). No wonder Peter became agitated when Jesus began to talk openly about suffering, rejection, and persecution. Mark 8:32 tells us that Peter finally took Jesus aside to straighten him out. He rebuked Jesus for having a negative attitude and for not continuing to capitalize on the momentum they had picked up during the most recent days of extraordinary miracles and large crowds.

Jesus' response is strong as he fires back at Peter in front of the other disciples, "Get behind me, Satan. You do not have in mind the things of God but the things of men" (Mark 8:33, NIV). Here lies the first key to unlocking and ultimately overcoming obsession: We need to change our minds.

Changing Our Minds

Albert Einstein is reported to have said, "I want to think the thoughts of God. All else is trivia." At first it sounds presumptuous and slightly intimidating to assume that we know God's thoughts. Yet it is possible if we allow God to lead us on a daily basis.

To have in mind God's things rather than people's things demands that we ask fresh questions and make new choices. Too often my choices are predictable and boring. I play it safe and react to the world around me without taking time to listen for God's leading. My knee-jerk responses are probably keeping God at a distance instead of opening the door for an intimate relationship.

Is it possible to know what God wants in particular circumstances? Scripture makes clear that we can and should have "the mind of Christ" in our daily lives. God has revealed himself in Scripture to those who desire to know him. He has come to earth as a person called Jesus to live among us and demonstrate who God is in tangible ways. Finally, we have the Holy Spirit, alive within us, to help us understand and act in wisdom as God leads us forward into uncertain times. Yes, we can know the thoughts of God if we are willing to change our minds.

Worrying. Think for a moment about how you handle times of change and transition. These tend to be particularly stressful for most of us. How are we to think during this time? Some people use this as opportunity to obsess. We can fall into the trap of worrying. "What will happen to me? What if I don't like the changes or final outcome? What if I make a mistake and make wrong choices? What if. . . ."

I recently moved across country with my family and found myself feeling the gnawing presence of stress. The sheer weight of details, possible mishaps, and uncertainty about the future kept crushing down on me. In the middle of the move, it dawned on me that my life (and the move) were way beyond my control.

One evening while talking about the complexity of the move, a friend asked me, "Do you have to obsess? Isn't there another option?" Just then, I realized how I fall into the trap of obsessive worry without taking time to choose a different response or reaction to my situation. I will always have stress of various intensity, but I don't have to continue to worry.

Campaigning. While some people react with worry, others are more proactive; they respond to stress by acting like campaigners. They become a whirlwind of motion and action, hoping to influence or control the outcome. They may frantically lobby to have their solution or goal achieved. Believing that they know the right strategy to follow, they campaign and promote to get others to agree with them.

Turtling. Still other people react to the stress inherent in change by withdrawing or being passive and guarded. I call this response *turtling*. My son Damian has a turtle named Charley. I would not be exaggerating to say he is not the most exciting pet. Most of the time he sits under a towel with his head, arms, and legs pulled into his shell, waiting for a safe time to come out of hiding.

Some of us, though committed Christians, tend to be spiritual turtles. Sometimes I find myself turtling even though I should know better. Under pressure I withdraw, hold back, watch, and wait until decisions are made and directions are chosen. Then I determine, if they please me, to stick my head out and look around.

All three reactions are very human. Worriers, campaigners, and turtlers are common enough that we are not surprised to find them in the Christian community. But none of them represents the thoughts of God.

Changing our minds requires that we resist the tendency to follow our natural approaches. We begin with prayer that aligns us with God's agenda, rather than prayer that tries to convince him of what we have already decided. Then we ask quite simply that he show us the kind of people he wants to see emerge from the shadows and experiences of our lives. What kind of men and women and children of faith are we nurturing in our lives and in our churches?

We ask what kind of participation it will take to nurture, encourage, and build the people who are products of our shared worship and ministry. Then we ask how we can equip ourselves to be effective ministers of the gospel and builders of people.

We can break obsession when we open ourselves to God's fresh, new presence and purpose in our lives. We are not doomed to go through the same old things. When we have in mind the things of God and not the things of people, we can be renewed even in times of transition and change.

Letting Go

"Whoever wants to save his life will lose it, but whoever loses his life for me and for the gospel will save it. What good is it for a person to gain the whole world, yet forfeit his soul?" (Mark 8:35–36, NIV).

Jesus' words in this passage are disturbing, but they point us to a way out of the obsession trap. Victory over obsession begins when we choose to let go. Because of my natural controlling tendencies, I have to work at releasing my grip on people, projects, dreams, programs, even relationships. While at meetings, the dentist's office, or church services, I sometimes realize that my hands are clenched tightly. It is as if I am holding on to an invisible aspect of my life.

I have learned a little exercise that helps me let go. I shake my hands free. After all, it is very difficult to remain tense, uptight, and worried when my hands are relaxed. A friend who coached track said she always taught her students to run with their hands loose so that no extra energy was spent clenching their fists. Believe me, if you start shaking your hands loose the next time you feel tense in church, those around you may think it a little odd, but you will begin to relax a bit.

When we come up against obstacles, decisions, or important unresolved issues, Jesus reminds us to let them go. If we hold on to them, we will lose in the long run.

Another key to overcoming obsession is deciding what is most important. Jesus asks, "What does it profit a person to gain the whole world and lose his soul?" Many of us go through our lives without consciously considering what is most important. Why do we make the choices we make? Is there a purpose behind our actions, or do we merely react to whatever jumps out at us each day?

Our faith gives us the power and the courage to be intentional even in the face of our most difficult situations. But even if I make the choices that release me from obsession, circumstances change and life pulls the rug out from under me. How can I learn to trust God while going through difficult circumstances?

CHAPTER THREE

Overcoming Circumstances

There was never yet a philosopher that could endure
the toothache patiently.
WILLIAM SHAKESPEARE

You meant evil against me; but God meant it for good.
GENESIS 50:20

I'M learning from some of the teenagers in my life that
there are three essential questions to be asked in any circumstance: Why?, Why not?, and Why me? Sometimes I think that if
we could figure out the answers to these questions, we would
have a handle on overcoming circumstances.

On "Cheers," Norm walks into the bar and is asked, "How's
life, Norm?" "It's a dog-eat-dog world," he responds, "and I'm
wearing milkbone underwear." Perhaps that's a little bit of what
Joseph in the book of Genesis felt as he looked back on his life.
The story of this biblical figure is actually very contemporary. The
issues and struggles he faced are in many ways the same circumstances that most of us deal with in our own lives.

He had been the favorite son. As is often the case in dysfunctional families, his father, Jacob, not only loved Joseph more
than the other sons, but he made his preference clear to all the

other siblings. Chapter 37 of Genesis says that because of this his brothers hated him and would not even speak to him in a peaceful way.

For Joseph, things went steadily downhill. His brothers plotted to kill him but, at the last minute, rescinded and instead sold him into slavery to a band of travelling merchants. As a slave, he prospered and grew in responsibility, but he was soon the victim of sexual harassment at the workplace. When he refused to participate in the seduction, he lost his job and was sent to prison.

Wasting away in prison, Joseph befriended two officers of the King's court who promised to gain his release. But when they were freed, they forgot Joseph and left him to suffer in prison for two more years before they remembered and released him.

In time he even became rich, powerful, and successful, serving in Pharaoh's court. He was instrumental in forecasting times of prosperity and famine. He devised a central storage system for the country so that the people would be able to withstand and survive the difficulties of the lean years. Ultimately he was reunited with his family, and the broken relationships were restored.

The Truths About Circumstances

It is possible to learn from Joseph's experiences and discover some truths about circumstances of life that will help us to live more effectively.

Circumstances are often the result of human choice as well as natural forces. At each turning point in Joseph's experience, people made choices, considered options, and took action. His circumstances were not impersonal acts of nature, a cosmic force, or "the dark side" we hear about in the *Star Wars* movies. Rather, people chose to act or react in various ways that created the circumstances of his life.

John Boykin describes the origins of World War I in *Stanford Magazine*. He says, "Planning for war assumed its own momentum [until] in 1914, military expediency dominated the decision-making process, and *war declared itself.*"

He goes on to say, "There is nothing wrong with saying for the sake of convenience that things happen, but we all know perfectly well that crime does not rise and that war does not declare itself. People commit crimes and people declare war. Whatever happens is the direct result of decisions people make and things people do."

It is easy to see circumstances as impersonal events that happen to us. But there is often a very human connection. When we see this, we also can begin to see ways that circumstances can be overcome.

Difficulties can be a great leveler of humanity, for no one is immune. Tim Hansel is a friend who grew up in the Seattle area and is the founder of Summit Expeditions, a wilderness survival school. In his book *You Gotta Keep Dancin'*, he wrote, "Perhaps God gives us difficulties in order to give us the opportunity to know who we really are and who we really can be. We live in a world that is sometimes constipated by its own superficiality. But life's difficulties are even a privilege, in that they allow us or force us to break through the superficiality to the deeper life within."

After moving into our new home, my wife, Eileen, and I tried to figure out how to get to know our neighbors. Though they were friendly and polite, it was hard to break through and become friends. This all changed one morning when I heard a knock on the door and was surprised to see my neighbor with a very upset look on his face.

"You'd better come out here," he said. Then I saw it. His two-year-old child had put his truck in gear and rolled it backwards down the hill, smashing into two of my cars and plowing them into the garage door.

I think I showed incredible grace under pressure as I politely checked to see that the baby was safe before I inspected the damage to my totalled sports car and the brand new family car that was smashed apart. At that moment, I could have thrown a fit, said something appropriately mean for the situation, or made any number of worthwhile reactions to the disaster. Instead, I laughed and said, "Hi, my name is John. I'm your new neighbor." We would never have planned it this way, but our wish came true. That accident was the beginning of a great friendship.

We cannot choose our circumstances, but we can choose our responses. If anyone had grounds to be miserable, bitter, discouraged, angry, cynical, or depressed, it was Joseph. Who says he wasn't? After all, it is hard to go through tough times. I am sure he struggled with these feelings and more as he faced setback after setback of unfair and unjust circumstances.

Perhaps his mind swirled with thoughts of how he might have responded differently in each situation. "If only . . . ," "What if . . . ?," and other ideas might have come to him as he found himself in a spiral of discouraging circumstances.

Did he have regrets? Of course. Were there things he could have done differently? Perhaps. Did he have the power to choose how he would respond in each situation? Absolutely! Joseph could have given up in defeat or become embittered and sullen. He could have chosen vengeance on the family that betrayed him. He could have used his power and position to guarantee that he would never be vulnerable again.

But in Genesis 50, he chooses to respond with grace. He had a right to be hard. He had the power to give his brothers what they deserved, but he chose to give them the one thing no one deserves—grace. "So do not fear; I will provide for you and your little ones. Thus he reassured them and comforted them" (Gen. 50:21).

It is easy to feel powerless over how we respond to circumstances. That is understandable. Choosing how we will respond is not easy but it is possible.

Tim Hansel also says in *You Gotta Keep Dancin'*, "Pain is inevitable, but misery is optional. We cannot avoid pain, but we can avoid joy. . . . I know people who spend their entire lives practicing being unhappy, diligently pursuing joylessness. They get more mileage from having people feel sorry for them than from choosing to live out their lives in the context of joy.

Tim writes, "At any moment in life we have at least two options, and one of them is to choose an attitude of gratitude, a posture of grace, a commitment to joy."

Lest you think Tim is someone who doesn't know what he's talking about, he lives in constant pain as the result of a fall while mountain climbing in the Sierras. His book is a challenge to choose joy in the midst of pain.

Recently I heard about a woman on the east coast named Kathleen Gooley who in face of a very painful circumstance chose grace. When the groom backed out of her wedding and left her with a $4,500 reception bill, the jilted bride decided to have a party anyway—for the area's poor. She sent notices to nearby shelters inviting 150 homeless people to her reception. Busloads of homeless men, women, and children arrived at the decorated catering hall. Many hadn't had a hot meal in weeks.

Gooley, dressed in black with a corsage pinned to her blouse, laughed and danced, saying that in spite of some misgivings about the day, she was glad she chose to do something positive. She said that one reason she had the party was because she and one of her children, then a baby, spent a night in a shelter twenty-three years ago. Kathleen had the courage to turn a potentially devastating circumstance into a party.

God's intention is for good. When faced with painful circumstances, it is easy to blame or resent God. How could a loving God allow this to happen to me? Why do bad things happen to good people? Where was God when I needed him? It is easy to wonder why God allows so much hurt in our lives.

Joseph, for all of the pain, failure, and eventual success, somehow understood that while people have mixed motives and cannot be trusted, God's intention for his children is good. And he can be trusted to overcome the worst circumstances that life brings to us. I've read a number of books that assume that God causes things to happen to us. We will probably never know why disasters come along with such regularity. But we can know what Joseph discovered—that God will make something good out of our lives.

Sometimes this is difficult for us to realize at first appearance because we usually cannot see God's purposes in the thick of the circumstances. It is only as we look back in hindsight that we catch a glimmer of how God worked for good in the midst of our circumstances.

I think one of the most useless responses we make to someone who is going through tough times is to ask, "What is God teaching you through this?" Equally galling is the presumption that we can suggest a greater purpose for another's suffering. These responses don't take seriously the fact that pain hurts and that healing is a process.

Perhaps our desire to identify something good in the midst of bad circumstances is a deep-seated insecurity or doubt about God's ability to handle our lives. Do we really need to protect his reputation or defend his good name in the face of legitimate questions and very real hurt?

"I'm trying to be a good example and encourage people in their faith," a young executive told me over lunch. "I'm afraid if they knew how bad my life is right now that they might turn away from God. I feel like I have to keep up the image of being a

happy, successful Christian, or I'll let them down. Besides, if I'm
honest with my Christian friends, they'll just try and talk me out
of my anger and frustration, or make me feel guilty for not feeling better. But that doesn't help; it only makes it worse."

As he shared his frustration, I thought of the times I put on
a front rather than being honest with others. I needed to remember that God doesn't need my efforts to protect him; he wants
my love and trust in the midst of life's circumstances. It is only as
I go through difficult times and prosperous times, trying times
and whimsical times, that I discover his abiding love and care for
me. At those times I learn that his intention is for good and that
he was there all the time. I can then affirm, like Joseph, "You
meant evil against me, but God meant it for good" (Gen. 50:20).

The Psalmist wrote: He "redeems my life from the pit"
(Psalm 103:4). I like that because the visual image is that God
does more than save my soul; he also saves me from my circumstances. Whether my pain is self-inflicted through sin or stupidity
or imposed by the hurt that others cause, his grace brings re-
demption.

Paul realized this when he wrote from prison, in Philippians:
"I want you to know, brethren, that what has happened to me
has really served to advance the gospel, so that it has become
known throughout the whole praetorian guard and to all the rest
that my imprisonment is for Christ; and most of the brethren
have been made confident in the Lord because of my imprisonment, and are much more bold to speak the word of God without fear" (Phil. 1:12–14).

The future is unknown, but it is secure.   Putting our lives in
Jesus' hands and trusting him to be both our savior and Lord
gives us confidence that we can trust him in a very uncertain
future. But it doesn't necessarily mean that we will know or control all circumstances that lie ahead of us. If we know what is
ahead, we don't need to live moment-to-moment by faith alone.

Genesis ends with Joseph dying a peaceful man, sure that his family was secure and the future lay bright before them. But life isn't a happily-ever-after experience this side of heaven. If you turn the page you see Exodus 1:8, "Now there arose a new king over Egypt, who did not know Joseph." And the troubles rekindled in earnest.

But every circumstance becomes an opportunity to experience God's saving grace at the point of our greatest need. In the process we overcome even the most hurtful circumstances.

I received a letter from a beautiful woman in our church who with her husband faces the pain of childlessness. She says, "After nearly five years of actively 'trying' and wanting to have a child, I sometimes look back and still can't believe it. It all seems like a very long bad dream. Sometimes I hope I'll wake up and have all of this be over. But then, I realize again, that it is true: I will never experience pregnancy; I will never breast-feed my child; I will never bear a child that my husband and I made together. The losses feel tremendous to me; I will never be the same. Many of my dreams stemming from when I was a young girl have been shattered."

She then describes some of her pain that wells up at unexpected times such as the first day of school, when she watches a baptism in church, or when a commercial flashes on television. She feels broken emotionally, worn out physically, and stretched to the point where her anger led her to the brink of walking away from her faith.

Well-meaning friends told her to "just trust God and he will provide." But she knew it wasn't that simple because it implies that trusting makes the pain evaporate, or that God will end up giving you what you ask. It simply didn't work that way for her.

"To trust God in the midst of pain, anguish, unanswered prayer, and loss, is a minute-by-minute battle. It means trusting God in the face of my pain. It means trusting God even though he may not give me what I ask. It means choosing to love him

even if it costs you the loss of a part of you. But, the trust and relationship with Christ brings meaning and hope to the pain.

"I guess the bottom line for me is that God holds us. He
holds us in our pain. He holds us in our joy. When we are broken
without an ounce of faith or trust, he holds us. When we feel like
leaving him, or even choose to walk away, he holds us. He
doesn't leave. And his tremendous grace draws us to him. . . . It's
this grace of our Lord that gives us peace when there's no earthly
reason to feel it."

These words are a powerful reminder that even in the worst
of circumstances we can find grace to sustain us and take us a step
further.

In the movie *Children of a Lesser God,* a young deaf woman
explains how she has gotten through the difficult, sometimes
painful circumstances of her life. Slowly she signs, "I've discovered that even when I hurt, I won't blow away."

Grace is God's provision to let us know that when we hurt,
we will not blow away. We can move forward and overcome our
circumstances. But it is still hard to handle difficult circumstances
when those around me appear to be doing a whole lot better.

CHAPTER FOUR

Overcoming Envy

The spirit he caused to live in us envies intensely . . . but he gives us more grace.
JAMES 4:5, 6, NIV

"*EVERY* time a friend succeeds," Gore Vidal has said, "I die a little." At first it sounds a little harsh and unloving, but the more I think about it, the more I realize that he speaks for all of us who struggle with jealousy and envy. For centuries envy has raised its head and drawn people into a malaise of conflict and discontent. Even some of the most powerful characters in the Bible found themselves caught in the grip of envy.

I suspect King Saul was crazy. He seems so erratic and self-destructive in the biblical account of his life that there is very little common ground to compare ourselves with him. As a young man, Saul was chosen to be the first king of the Israel nation. He had everything: power, intelligence, glamour, riches, and the love and respect of his people. Yet in spite of all these things, he began to act like a certifiable wild man. There are probably grounds to consider him paranoid with manic-depressive mood swings.

At first glance it seems that we are not like him. In our eyes, it is pretty apparent that we are the solid citizens. We are the prosperous, successful, and the secure. We are educated, cultured, socialized, analyzed, blessed, and dressed for success. Saul, on the other hand, was a rascal and an unlovable character. Though it may not seem so on the surface, we have more in common with Saul than we think.

Saul's reign as King of Israel began in envy. The Old Testament first book of Samuel provides an account in which, following a great victory over their enemies, the people rose up and demanded that God give them a king. The elders came to Samuel and said, "You are old, and your sons do not walk in your ways; now appoint a king to lead us, such as all the other nations have" (1 Sam. 8:5, NIV).

The people wanted to turn away from that which God had given them, leave behind the things that made them unique and different among the nations, and pursue their neighbors' possessions. This was the seedbed into which Saul was anointed king.

The Lord tells Samuel, "They have not rejected you, but they have rejected me from being king over them. According to all the deeds which they have done to me, from the day I brought them up out of Egypt even to this day, forsaking me and serving other gods, so they are also doing to you" (1 Sam. 8:7, 8).

As I study the account of Saul's rise to power, I see a shy, gifted, physically strong young man with basically good intentions and an unwillingness to submit his will to become obedient to the Lord.

Time and again he finds himself on the brink of faithfulness, only to divert his eyes for an instant to see what others are doing, thinking, or getting. In that instant he succumbs to envy and falls away from God. His envy leads to fear, which leads to resentment, rage, and finally self-destruction.

Forms of Envy

When I was young, our family joined the Jewish Community Center in the town where we lived. It was a wonderful place filled with creative activities and opportunities to meet new friends. Of course, as the only *goyim* in the center, we probably seemed like a bit of an oddity to the other members.

It wasn't long before most of my friends were Jewish, and it wasn't a problem until their bar mitzvahs. First Richard Novick, then Michael Goldenstein, finally John Sussmann celebrated this special ceremony signifying the turn to manhood.

I attended each ceremony, brought gifts, and stayed late into the night at the obligatory parties. But as each of my friends turned thirteen and had their party, I began to resent them because I was not going to be bar mitzvahed. I would have no party, special ceremony, gifts, or envelopes of money from distant uncles and aunts. There would be no fantastic kosher buffet from Blummer's Bakery and no magical line that I'd cross over into manhood. I found myself filled with envy and resentment, not because of their good fortune but because I wanted it, too.

I want what they want. Envy takes many subtle forms in our lives. It is rooted in our desires, but it is ultimately demonstrated in our relationships. The first form of envy is "I want what they want." The key element of this form of envy is to allow the desires of other people to determine our own desires.

When we succumb to this kind of envy, we submit our will not to God or the Lordship of Jesus Christ but to the cult of popular opinion. When in doubt, take a public-opinion poll! Go with the crowd. When this happens in a church, we begin to practice lowest-common-denominator Christianity. The Bible warns us in James 4 that "anyone who chooses to be a friend of the world becomes an enemy of God" (James 4:4, NIV). What others want must never be the determining factor for followers of Jesus Christ.

Saul seemed to care more about his image before the people than he did about his relationship with God. When Samuel confronts him with his disobedience and sin, Saul responds, "I was afraid of the people and so I gave in to them" (1 Sam. 15:24, NIV). Then he tries to persuade Samuel to return with him to make an appearance together at worship. At first Samuel refuses, but Saul begs him, "I have sinned, but please honor me before the elders of my people and before Israel, come back with me, that I may worship the Lord your God" (1 Sam. 15:30, NIV).

Like most of us, Saul was probably at heart a people pleaser. Appearances mattered more to him than godliness. He found himself more worried about how he appeared to people than how he appeared to God. His priorities were out of line. This desire to please and to win the approval of others can render us spiritually impotent and unable to move forward in our relationship with Christ.

When we allow ourselves to be unduly influenced by other's opinions, we can find ourselves overlooking the very wonderful blessings that are right in front of us. I came across a poem called "Mother of the Bride" that describes a young bride and her mother shopping for the perfect wedding outfits. In every shop, with every sales lady, the mother gleefully exclaimed, "My daughter is getting married to a lawyer. A junior partner at his firm." Day after day this went on in shop after shop, until the young bride revealed "never once did mother mention that I was a lawyer too."

Unfortunately there are times when we are so eager to impress and win the approval of others that we unthinkingly neglect or demean those we love in the process.

I want what they have. The second form of envy is "I want what they have." Saul's envy of David grew until he was filled with a murderous brooding rage because David had something that Saul desired. David seemed to have everything: success, power, accolades, abilities, good looks, popularity, and spiritual depth. "When Saul saw how successful [David] was, he was afraid of him" (1 Sam. 18:15, NIV).

Have you ever felt threatened or frightened by someone else's success? If we are honest with ourselves, we can say that we all have felt this way. One Greek philosopher said, "Few people have the natural strength to honor a friend's success without envy." Even though I am committed to my friends' success and wish them well, I tend to feel a biting twinge of envy when they do *too* well.

The biblical warnings against coveting, or what Bruce Larson calls "looking over your neighbor's fence," get to the heart of our struggle with envy. It is almost as if we don't know that we are living without until we see what "the Joneses" have. Then we feel like the "have nots."

"I didn't know how shabby my furniture was until I visited your house now I'm disgusted with our home." "I was content with my salary until I found out what others were paid. Now I feel cheated by the company." "I liked my comfortable old sweater until I found out I looked like a flabby Mr. Rogers. Now I want to burn this old rag." These comments and others all resonate with the reality of envy.

A whole world of marketing has been developed to create the sense that we are missing something or that we are out of it if we don't get the newest things. We all are susceptible to this form of pressure.

One week, as I was having my broken-down 1969 Buick towed into the garage . . . for the third time . . . after the starter

went out again . . . on Thanksgiving weekend . . . in a rainstorm
. . . , I admit that I had impure thoughts about my car, and I
confess that I looked with a degree of greedy lust at some of the
newer cars on the road that had starters that worked . . . even in
the rain. It was a small consolation to mutter under my breath,
"Just wait twenty years and your car will be like mine!" I wanted
what they had.

I want what they are. The third form of envy is, "I want what
they are." Woody Allen says, "My greatest regret in life is that
I'm not someone else." We can laugh at that, but there is a
creeping uncertainty that pulls at our hearts as if to ask, wouldn't
it be a lot easier if I could be like them? Of course, we know that
it wouldn't be easier because the premise is based on the false as-
sumption that others must have it better and easier than we. We
know it isn't true, but we still find ourselves longing to be what
they are.

The poem "Richard Cory" by Edwin Arlington Robinson
shocks us with the reminder that below our well-polished exteri-
ors can be a sea of personal turmoil and pain.

> Whenever Richard Cory went downtown,
> We people on the pavement looked at him;
> He was a gentleman from sole to crown,
> Clean favored, and imperially slim.
>
> And he was always quietly arrayed,
> And he was always human when he talked;
> But still he fluttered pulses when he said,
> "Good morning," and he glittered when he walked.
>
> And he was rich—yes, richer than a king—
> And admirably schooled in every grace;
> In fine, we thought that he was everything
> To make us wish that we were in his place.

So on we worked, and waited for the light,
And went without the meat, and cursed the bread;
And Richard Cory, one calm summer night,
Went home and put a bullet through his head.

Envy blinds us to the real world and taunts us into lusting after the life of our neighbor. In the process we end up fearing, resenting, and perhaps even hating them because of who they are and because we are not them. Perhaps this is how Saul felt as he jealously watched young David. The Bible points out that "Saul was afraid of David because the Lord was with David but had left Saul" (1 Sam 18:12, NIV).

How can we overcome envy when it rises up in our hearts, clouds our thoughts, and imperils our relationships? When I am envious, I'm tempted to either justify my envy or deny it and pretend that it isn't there.

If we are to overcome envy, we must resist the urge to either *express* or *repress* the feelings within us. James 3:14 says, "But if you harbor bitter envy and selfish ambition in your hearts, *do not boast about it or deny the truth*" (NIV, italics mine).

Expressers drive me crazy. They always let you know exactly what they are feeling at any given time. They hold nothing back. Sometimes I am afraid to ask expressers how they are doing for fear of having them open a huge bag of emotional garbage and unload it on my unsuspecting head.

Expressers are particularly fond of justifying their particular situation. When I fall into the expresser trap, I blame others for my misfortune and defend the rightness of my position. This tends to make me a very annoying companion. I yell when I am angry, howl when I am wronged, stamp my foot when I feel ignored, and somehow manage to find new ways to be offended.

When we defend our self-centeredness and dress it up in trappings of acceptable behavior or put it in a book with a catchy title such as *Looking Out for Number One, Winning Through Intimidation,* or *Having It All in a Have-Not World,* we can blind ourselves to God's truth and deny his power in our lives.

People who suppress are very different. They will try to hold in their feelings. They deny that there is anything wrong and most likely will put on the martyr mask. I like being with friends who tend to suppress. They are often quiet, good listeners, and rarely unload on anyone. But they can do damage to themselves.

To suppress the truth requires great intestinal fortitude because in spite of the pressure building within and the evidence growing on the surface, they strive to maintain control and act as though there is nothing wrong. Their motto becomes "Keep a lid on it."

Before we had microwave ovens, the way to cook things fast was to utilize the trusty pressure cooker. I used one with great skill, and I could boil potatoes in twenty or thirty minutes and make beef stew in an hour. The heat had to be regulated by watching a small pressure valve that rocked on the top of the sealed lid.

One night I was putting together a pretty elegant beef stew when I forgot to regulate the heat on the cooker and left it on the stove while I became engrossed in a television show. In a desperate attempt to make up for my negligence, I forgot to cool down the lid and instead turned the handle to open the pressure cooker. What an explosion! There was stew blown throughout the kitchen and dining room of our little apartment. It was clinging to the ceiling and running down the cupboards.

When we deny the truth about the envy within us, we can become like the pressure cooker. We try to keep a lid on it, but it builds up until we feel as if we will explode.

Neither expressing nor repressing will bring the health we need. We need to take hold of an old word that at first seems very out of date and infuse it with new meaning. That word is *confess,* and in it lies our hope for overcoming envy. It is only when we confess our envy and allow ourselves and a few others to see the truth about our attitudes and behaviors that we discover freedom to live released from the grip of envy.

Confession acknowledges, "This is my problem, not yours; please forgive me." It opens the doors for healing in our broken relationships and allows us to loosen our grip on things and people in our lives. It also opens us to receive grace.

I love the reminder from James 4:5, 6: "The spirit that he caused to live in us envies intensely, but he gives us more grace" (NIV). When we receive the gift of grace, we no longer have to remain trapped in the bitter cycle of envy; we receive more grace. When we feel left out and lonely, we receive more grace. When we feel overlooked and underappreciated, we receive more grace. When those less-qualified, and less-committed, are honored above us, we receive more grace. When life is not fair . . . , when people are cruel . . . , when grief overwhelms us . . . , when burdens seem endless . . . , when evil ones prosper . . . , when dreams are shattered . . . , when our lives are broken and we think they will never be whole again . . . , he gives more grace. More grace. . . . More grace!

CHAPTER FIVE

Overcoming Temptation

I can resist everything except temptation.
OSCAR WILDE

He was tempted in every way like us.
HEBREWS 4:15 (PARAPHRASE)

I learned about temptation the old-fashioned way: I tripped over it. As a teenager, my main interest and passion, besides girls, was playing guitar in a rock and roll band. Our motto might have been, "If it's not good, at least it's loud." After practicing great hits of the sixties such as "Wild Thing" and "Louie Louie" over and over again, it was time for a meeting. We were scheduled to play for a big dance on the weekend, and we didn't have enough equipment to make a good impression. We also didn't have any money to buy or even rent anything from nearby Ozzie's Music Center where we liked to hang out.

Suddenly it came to me! An idea so brilliant, so simple, and so diabolical it had to work. I shared my plan with the other guys in the band, and while they seemed doubtful at first, it was obvious to everyone that this could really work. My plan was simple: We'd go into several churches in town when no one was around and steal their sound systems out of the sanctuaries. How could we miss? Every church had plenty of microphones, amplifiers, speakers, and wiring to equip most needy rock bands. So off we went.

Outside St. Luke's Lutheran Church, the drummer got cold feet and decided to stay in the car. The rest of us entered quietly, and we quickly unhooked their sound system and ran out to the car. My courage and confidence was soaring. We were unstoppable as we rode from church to church absconding with their equipment. Issues of right and wrong, ethical and moral absolutes faded away in the face of the onrushing force of adrenaline I experienced that afternoon in the great church-robbing caper.

But later that night, as I lay in bed thinking about the day, it suddenly occurred to me, "What have I done?" Then for the first time a wave of guilt swept over me and I knew I had blown it. The next day I took back the equipment to the churches, apologized to the various priests and pastors, and even paid to have everything rewired as it had been before we came along.

The band members had their own bouts of remorse and ended up telling their parents (emphasizing that it was all my idea). Then the parents wouldn't let their sons play with me, and the band broke up. We never played the big dance that weekend. I gave into temptation and lost what was most important to me at the time.

The Nature of Temptation

Temptation is probably one of the few things that all of us have in common. We are tempted in subtle and overt ways. We are tempted externally and internally. We are tempted at obvious times and when we least expect it. Mae West, the incredible philosopher in this century, commented, "I generally avoid temptation, unless I can't resist it."

As long as we live, there is a pretty good chance that we will be tempted. The issue for us is not how we keep from being tempted, for that is impossible. Rather we must deal with how we can resist temptation when it comes and avoid the self-destruction that seems to lurk continually in the shadows of our lives.

In the Bible, Matthew 4 shows us a glimpse at some of the temptations Jesus encountered as he began his ministry. Jesus understood the temptations we face, for he was fully human and subject to the same longings and frustrations.

In the gospel account, Jesus had just experienced a powerful and affirming event. He was baptized by his cousin, John, and the voice of God said, "This is my beloved Son, with whom I am well pleased" (Matt. 3:17). From this spiritual and emotional high, he was led into the wilderness where we are told he was tempted by Satan.

In our contemporary, secular world, it is easy to become confused about who our real enemy is. We secularize or socialize the problem hoping to reduce things to manageable size, but in the process we sometimes lose touch with reality. Sin is no longer disobedience to God; it becomes a social problem. When we lose sight of the spiritual reality of sin, we no longer seek forgiveness through repentance, but instead we try to treat the symptoms without addressing the underlying condition.

Unfortunately the treatment is only effective when there is a proper diagnosis of the problem. Paul understood this and reminds us in Ephesians 6:12, "For we are not contending against flesh and blood, but against the principalities, against the powers, against the world rulers of this present darkness. . . ."

Do you believe there is an enemy that seeks your downfall? Jesus did. Temptation does not exist in a vacuum. According to Scripture, its source lies in the action of one who would separate us from God, establish himself as the center of our universe, and ultimately destroy us with the lies and deception that are his tools.

It is okay to not believe in Satan or a personal evil, as the Bible repeatedly describes. But we can never have victory in our inner battles unless we come to grips with and understand the nature of our true enemy.

Deception. Temptation often begins with an element of deception. Perhaps this is why Scripture calls Satan "the father of lies." The deceit is often subtle but powerful. Whatever form it assumes, it usually begins with a challenge to our identity. "If you are the Son of God, command these stones to become loaves of bread" (Matt. 4:3).

There are a number of messages in this simple challenge: Prove yourself; you have a right to this. Meet your own needs on your own terms. Take control of your life to meet your needs. You are the center of your universe and have a right to be free from the gnawing hungers in your life. You should get what you crave or feel deprived of according to your own timetable, in your own way. God has abandoned you; he doesn't care about you or your pain. Therefore you must take things into your own hands.

When everything is going great, people tend to think they are above the lure of temptation. However, we are most subject to temptation at times following a great victory or positive experience or after times we have felt honored. We often feel invincible, strong, and successful. We also begin to feel that we actually deserve more or better, or different than everyone else. After all, don't we have it coming?

If we are subject to temptation when we are at the top, we are tempted even more so when we are at the bottom. When we feel deprived or alone, it is easy to slip into obsessive behaviors that allow us to focus solely on what is missing from our lives. Our unmet needs, our unfulfilled longings, and our lack of satisfaction with what is around us can lead to deep longings for what we think is lacking.

When our security and stability are threatened, when our world is in chaos, it is easy to feel confused, frightened, and even angry. We become very susceptible to temptation. There is the temptation to become distracted in our daily lives. We can be diverted from our calling to follow Christ, be deceived in our perceptions, and finally give up in despair at the overpowering sense of helplessness to make a difference in a world gone mad.

Our longing for satisfaction. We often run into temptation when we long for satisfaction. Everyone has needs. It does no good to tell yourself or someone else, "You shouldn't feel bad. Just think of those who are so much worse off than you." It is a meaningless comparison. There is always going to be someone worse off than you, and most likely someone better off as well. The issue is not how you compare. It is whether you will trust God regardless of your situation.

Noted psychologist Abraham Maslow showed us that as human beings we have a "hierarchy of needs." According to Maslow, we have basic needs such as shelter, food, and security. When these are met, however, we are still not satisfied. Instead we begin to experience a whole new level of needs: a need to love and be loved, to belong and feel part of a community bigger than ourselves. When these needs for love are met, we have need to express ourselves creatively and live meaningful lives with purpose and fulfillment.

This is nothing new; it has been in the Bible for a long time. Paul advised the early Church that they should not say to a hungry person, "I'll pray for you," or "Come to our Bible study" until they give that person something to eat. Paul realized that only when those basic needs were met could a person be open and aware of the other needs in his or her life.

It is insensitive and perhaps even rude to tell friends who are lonely and feeling unloved or unlovable to stop feeling sorry for themselves and begin to think of all the people in the world who are worse off than they. It is easy to assume that because a person has the outer signs of success that his or her needs for purpose and fulfillment are invalid. To dismiss the quiet yearning in a person who possesses great wealth but still longs for meaning diminishes his or her very legitimate needs. Those needs are every bit as valid as the more obvious needs such as safety, food, and shelter. God desires to meet us at the point of our need whether it is filling our stomachs, our hearts, or our minds. He is the one who satisfies every longing through his grace.

Jesus responds to the temptation to provide for his own obvious need for food by quoting from Deuteronomy 8:3, "Man shall not live by bread alone but from every word that comes from the mouth of the Lord" (NIV).

This Scripture reminds us that there is more to life than merely filling our stomachs, satisfying our cravings, and fulfilling our longings. There is a misconception or perhaps a deception that implies that we will be satisfied if our needs are met. But the satisfaction we pursue according to our own resources is an illusion and therefore not satisfaction.

Our longing for attention. Not only are we tempted to satisfy our personal needs. Temptation also strikes us where we are vulnerable—in the area of our pride and ego. "Then the devil took him to the holy city, and set him on the pinnacle of the temple, and said to him, "If you are the Son of God, throw yourself down; for it is written, 'He will give his angels charge of you,' and 'On their hands they will bear you up lest you strike your foot against a stone'" (Matt. 4:5, 6):

Satan can quote Scripture, too. By quoting Psalm 91:11, 12, Jesus is challenged by the father of lies to demonstrate in a powerful and dramatic manner that he is the Messiah. He would in an instant prove beyond a doubt, before the most devout worshippers in the most holy of all places, that he is God's promised Messiah. What better way to usher in the Kingdom of God? What better way to silence the critics, assure the doubters, and shame the scoffers? With this one dramatic gesture, Jesus could fulfill prophecy and satisfy the longing of the people in an instant. What could be wrong with that?

I know this temptation. In my work as a pastor, I'm confronted with the occupational hazard of trying to be a hero. Like metal drawn to a magnet, I'm drawn to people and situations that allow me to play God. Unfortunately, my way and God's way of doing things usually don't correlate too well. It is easy for me to come up with strategies and devise plans to help out in situations.

Slowly I'm learning that I have some mixed motives at work within me. Too often I find that I'm motivated by the lure of my ego to force God's hand. My own ego is working overtime to set myself up as a hero, to be loved and adored, to rescue the weak, and to provide answers to every question—to be seen as a spiritual giant who sacrifices for the little people. Perhaps you know this temptation, too.

The temptation to make ourselves look like heroes is perhaps the most dangerous of all. If Jesus circumvented the cross and established his kingdom through showmanship and miraculous proofs, there would be no need for faith. Even more, the kingdom would have been established without the cross. There would have been no atoning death and therefore no forgiveness for our sins. God's plan of salvation would have been diverted.

Our longing for power. The pursuit of power is a very real temptation. It affects us in our personal lives and business choices. It surfaces in marriage and family relationships and haunts our involvements in church. It pervades our finances and infiltrates our leisure. Power issues can be subtle or overt, but they are almost always destructive and insidious.

Jesus was tempted to take charge and satisfy the longing for power. "Again the Devil took him to a very high mountain, and showed him all the kingdoms of the world and the glory of them; and he said to him, "All these I will give you, if you will fall down and worship me." Then Jesus said to him "Begone, Satan! for it is written, 'You shall worship the Lord your God and him only shall you serve" (Matt. 4:8–10).

When someone we know comes into a position of power, we sometimes assume that he or she must have made a deal with the devil. Perhaps we sense at some deep level that there are no free lunches when it comes to power.

It is easy to despise those in history who symbolize power abuse at its worst. Adolph Hitler, Richard Nixon, Saddam Hussein, and others are easy targets for criticism because they represent a caricature of inappropriate uses of power. The message of this Scripture, however, is that apart from the grace of God we are all susceptible to the temptation to grasp and claw our way to the top of the corporate or social ladder, to gain the upper hand in relationships, and to be in charge of our individual worlds. There are marks of power gone wrong throughout our society, business, church, and families. They are etched in the face of greed, racism, discrimination, family strife, and war.

Jesus squarely faced the temptation to grasp power for himself. But as Carl Jung reminds us, "Where love rules, there is no will to power." Jesus resisted the will to power and allowed love to rule.

Overcoming Temptation

What can we do to overcome temptation? It is simple, but it won't be easy.

Expect it. One advantage I have in my life is that I am a confirmed, practicing pessimist. I go along expecting disaster at every turn. I call this an advantage because I've learned not to be surprised by problems or caught off guard by temptations. I've also come to see that being tempted is not a sin in itself. Temptation is (like the ads for Life Savers candy say) a part of living. It should be no surprise when we find ourselves tested, whether life is going great or whether we are struggling in the pits. We need to expect it and handle it when it comes our way.

Prepare for it. Prayer and meditation on God's word can help us withstand temptation when it comes. The Psalmist said, "Thy word have I hid in mine heart, that I might not sin against thee" (Psalm 119:11, KJV). Jesus responded to temptation with the words of Scripture. If we are ignorant of God's word, we lack the weapons to wage spiritual warfare. Likewise, prayer enables us to align ourselves with God's purposes and will, and we receive his strength for the battle.

Share it. The gospel writer tells us in Matthew 26 that Jesus faces his darkest hour before his death. He takes a few friends with him to pray while he agonizes about what is to come. Matthew records his words, "Watch and pray, that you may not enter into temptation. The spirit indeed is willing, but the flesh is weak" (Matt. 26:41).

Shared temptation loses its grip on us. But when we keep it to ourselves as our own problem to deal with in our own way, we begin to lose the battle. None of us can survive the temptations we face unless we are willing to open up and share the struggles with a few trusted friends. God's gift of commitments to accountable relationships keeps us healthy in a very unhealthy world.

Resist it. Many battles with temptation are lost simply because we don't put up a fight. Rather than being passive in the face of temptation, we can fight with all the power of heaven and earth at our disposal to aggressively resist the lure of temptation. We dare not give in out of boredom, discouragement, or complacency. Remember what Paul said: "Resist the devil and he will flee" (James 4:7).

PART II

Grace to Sustain

CHAPTER SIX

Grace and
Peace

What a fine fix we are in now; peace has been declared.
NAPOLEON BONAPARTE

Glory to God in the highest, and on earth peace among
people, with whom he is pleased.
LUKE 2:14

*W*hatever became of peace? As a child of the sixties, I
went to love-ins at our local park and spent evenings sitting in
coffeehouses listening to folksingers cry out for peace. In college
I joined in marches and demonstrated for peace and the end of
war. Peace was on our minds in campus dorms and apartments as
we gathered and talked long into the night about peace and the
state of our world. It all seemed terribly relevant at the time.

But something happened. Maybe the world changed, or
perhaps I did. People aren't excited about peace anymore. Even
the old two-finger peace sign is considered an obscene gesture in
some countries of the world. For some people, peace has even
become a joke. Comedian Jay Leno made us laugh when he
quipped, "As Miss America, my goal is to bring peace to the entire world and then to get my own apartment."

Whatever became of peace? It has been rendered trivial, dull, irrelevant, insignificant, impossible, impractical, unrealistic, and unattainable.

Peace is sometimes seen as the enemy of a successful growing economy (particularly in parts of our country where we depend on military contracts for jobs and income). When we face an economic downturn and the cutting back of our nation's war dollars, it is important to find an enemy somewhere in the world and crank up the war machine to bolster our employment, investment, manufacturing, and the military complex.

Peace may be overused and its vital meaning may be diluted to the point that it doesn't mean much to us anymore. But it is definitely rooted in our faith as Christians, and it should have great meaning for us. After all, we started it! We may not think very highly or very often about peace, but if the Bible is any indication, it is definitely on God's mind. Throughout the Bible we find references to peace and its possibilities in our lives.

When the angels gathered to announce Christ's birth, the word they brought was *peace*. Likewise, the prophet Isaiah told of the hope for the Messiah, "For to us a child is born, to us a son is given, and the government will be on his shoulder. And his name will be called 'Wonderful Counselor, Mighty God, Everlasting Father, Prince of Peace.' Of the increase of his government and of peace there will be no end" (Isa. 9:6–7).

In Scripture, peace is a marvelous word that is filled with meaning. The Hebrew word *Shalom,* which we hear frequently as a greeting, a blessing, and even a farewell, means "completeness or peaceful well-being." It is more than just prosperity and wealth; it is the wholeness that comes from being rooted and grounded in God's loving care.

The New Testament word for peace is *eirene.* It also communicates peace, but as a result of God's saving work to restore us to wholeness through our faith in Jesus Christ, not as merely the absence of conflict.

Jesus came to bring peace. It was the reason for his birth 2,000 years ago. But whatever became of peace? How did we end up missing God's gift of peace?

Misunderstandings About Peace

I try to know this peace, yet I continually misunderstand or miss the point that God seems to be trying to make. In order to know this peace, it may be helpful to see some of the misunderstandings we have about peace.

Peace is something we can attain through hard work and human effort. Some people think that peace is an attainable goal toward which we strive, rather than a natural outer expression of the inner transformation that is taking place within us.

In the state of Washington, where I used to live, we are very familiar with the sight of apple trees in little towns like Wenatchee and Yakima. Are these apple trees trying with all of their might to generate apples? Of course not. Trees don't have to work and strain to produce their fruit. If they are healthy and growing, the fruit will appear naturally. Likewise, peace is the natural result of the Holy Spirit's activity in our lives. It will be produced in us without our frantic attempts to generate it or make it happen. It is a free gift from God to us.

Perhaps this is why grace and peace are so often linked together in Scripture. Grace is God's attitude of unrelenting love and acceptance. It doesn't deal with us according to what we deserve, but according to his unending mercy. Peace is the experience we have when we accept God's free gift of grace.

The lack of peace in our lives and in our world may be partly the result of our unwillingness to receive and extend grace. If we insist on getting what we deserve and keeping balanced accounts of what we have coming and what others owe us, we will never know the peace that comes from living day-to-day and moment-by-moment in grace.

Peace can be obtained through strength, power, or strong defenses. Those who believe this presume that peace is the result of gaining the upper hand against any and all who would threaten us. "I thoroughly disapprove of duels," Mark Twain once said. "If a man should challenge me, I would take him kindly and forgivingly by the hand and lead him to a quiet place and kill him."

No matter how well we are defended or how strong we are, peace still alludes us. We will never be rich enough, strong enough, or tough enough to acquire the peace we crave. We must always stay alert and ready for the next challenger. We must always be planning our next defense.

The great boxer Muhammed Ali understood what many of us have failed to recognize. He said, "When you can whip any man in world, you never know peace."

There can be peace apart from God. We have become somewhat expert in our attempts to segment our lives and compartmentalize the way we live. This practice works against us when it comes to finding wholeness.

We keep God in the religion box. Peace belongs under relationships, politics, or perhaps, retirement. It is important to allow God to involve himself in every area of life. He doesn't want to be confined to a religious compartment that would bore him. We lose something when we forget that peace is not possible apart from God's loving intervention in our daily lives. In a real sense, it is a miracle.

In Luke 2:14, the angel announced, "Glory to God in the highest and on earth peace to all those with whom he is pleased." We can see from this passage that glory to God and peace on earth are inseparably linked. When we give glory to God, we begin to experience peace, for our perspective starts to align with our creator's.

Peace is not for everyone. Some people prefer the turmoil or fight to stay in control rather than allow the peace of God to permeate their lives. Certainly it is available freely to everyone, but it is only attainable for those who receive the free gift of grace offered in Jesus Christ. Without Christ, there can be no peace!

There can be no peace within, for we are out of synch with our true selves. Though we are made in God's image, meant to live in relationship with him, we have not yet yielded control of our lives to him. In the meantime we frantically search, trying anything and everything that will help us discover the peace for which we long.

Every week I meet with women and men who say they need to "find themselves." Complaining that something is wrong inside or in their relationships, marriage, or work, they don't feel whole or peaceful. Sometimes they think the problem is with the others in their life. "If I was married to someone else. . . . If I was only married. . . . If I could just get out of this marriage. . . . If I worked for a different company. . . . If I worked for any company. . . . If I could just quit working all together." You know what I'm talking about.

As they share some of the pieces of their struggle, it often rings true for me as well. I find myself wondering what my life would be like if I had made different choices along the way. Usually in hindsight I'm grateful for my life, my experiences, and the way things are turning out. But there are plenty of failures, embarrassments, and empty spots to remind me that I am still on the journey and I certainly have not arrived yet. Despite my best intentions, I am well aware of a gnawing emptiness deep inside me that cries out to be filled.

Mathematician Blaise Pascal described the "God-shaped vacuum that is within every person." We may try our best to fill it and create a sense of well-being and peace, but it can only be filled by the one who made us and knows us and loves us. Jesus says, "Peace I leave with you; my peace I give unto you; not as the world gives. . . . Let not your hearts be troubled, neither let them be afraid" (John 14:27).

Until we say yes to Christ and put our lives into his care, the chasm that keeps us alienated, distant, and unpeaceful cannot be crossed. Our relationships will continue to be marred by discord and tension; our world will be a place of stress and anxiety filled with enemies, both real and imagined, and our hearts will be restless and afraid.

How we end up at the end of our lives can sometimes be a reflection of how we lived. One possible scenario is portrayed in Randy Newman's sad poem "Old Man." It involves a young person at the bedside of an old friend: At the end of the visit, the young man reminds his friend that there will be no comforting God waiting for him. The old man had lived his whole life on his own terms: needing no one and being needed by no one. Now death was a sad and lonely exit.

This may be the peace that the world gives, but it is not the peace that Jesus gives. Let me tell you about a different ending. Our family recently made the trek to southern California to grieve and celebrate the homecoming of my wife's father.

Hilman had grown up on a rugged farm in North Dakota. He left the farm to join the marines because he had heard that life as a marine would be much easier than life as a farmer. It was, too. Though his last twenty years were spent physically debilitated with severe health problems, he had a vital faith and was learning to trust God on a daily basis.

One evening, in a conversation with Eileen's brother, he said, "I have been very afraid of dying. But today I was talking with the Lord about it, and I'm not afraid any more. Now I have peace." The next morning he went to be with his Lord. In the midst of a hard and troubled life, he discovered that peace is both very real and very possible.

CHAPTER SEVEN

Grace
and Hope

Sometimes wishing is the wings the truth comes true on.
And sometimes the truth is what sets us wishing for it.
FREDERICH BUECHNER

We have joy, because we know that suffering produces
perseverance; perseverance, character; and character
produces hope.
ROMANS 5:3 (PARAPHRASE)

I'M beginning to realize that in this world there are basically two kinds of people: those who can wait until Christmas to
open their presents and those who can't. I am a faithful waiter,
while my wife fits the second category. As a little girl she would
secretly take her presents away from the tree, open them to see
what was in them, then carefully rewrap and replace them under
the tree. Then on Christmas morning she would act very surprised as she opened her presents. Some years she could have
won a best actress Academy Award for her performance as the
surprised little girl.

In the early years of our marriage we had great arguments
about the relative merits of waiting to open our presents. I, of
course, was a purist who wanted to keep hope alive as long as
possible. She had to know at all costs. I think it was more impor-

tant for her to know than to experience the joy and tension that comes from experiencing hope.

If there is one time of year when hope is most visible, I think it is Christmas. There is the hope in the anticipation of a little child's face at the wonder of what may be under the tree. There is the anxious gleam in the eyes of the shopkeeper considering the potential profits of the season, and the abounding hope with every sale. Hope for our world grows as we place greater emphasis on goodwill, grace, and temporary cease-fire agreements.

There is hope in the hearts of family members as gatherings of clan rituals take place with fervor. Perhaps this year will be different. Maybe the family will get along and try to be loving for a few hours or days so we can get through the holidays. And there is spiritual hope abounding. In rest homes, neighborhoods, churches, and hospitals, messages of hope are delivered and received as hopeful carols are sung:

> How silently, how silently, the wondrous gift is given.
> So God imparts to human hearts the blessings of his heaven.
> No ear may hear his coming,
> But in this world of sin,
> Where meek souls will receive him,
> Still the dear Christ enters in.

Christmas has always been a season of hope. Jesus fulfilled the hopes and longings of a people 2,000 years ago. And he fulfills our hopes and longings even today.

The Meaning of Hope

What is hope? And why is it such a necessary and valued treasure in our lives today? One wise person said, "Hope is the feeling you have that the feeling you have isn't permanent."

The Greek word for hope in the New Testament is *elpis*. It is used as a noun or verb, not an adjective or adverb. Those of you who are English teachers know what this means. The words *hopeful* and *hopefully* are too subjective—too dependent on circumstances or personal feelings. The hope of the Christian faith is always concrete and objective. It is not determined by our moods or predicaments. This is important because it is easy to think of hope as a mild, tepid form of wishful thinking. A feeling or mood that we have to conjure up in our own minds.

There is nothing wrong with wishful thinking. Dreamers are always in short supply. I still remember the lilting voice of Jiminy Cricket reminding us that "when you wish upon a star, makes no difference who you are, your dreams come true." I used to wonder why, if that song was true, my life couldn't be more like a perpetual visit to Disneyland.

Hope in the Bible is not a vague longing or blurred possibility. It is both real and reasonable. Thus the apostle Paul can say, "Be ready to give a reason for the hope that is within you."

The Foundation and Source of Hope

What is the concrete foundation of our hope? One great hymn announces:

> My hope is built on nothing less
> than Jesus' blood and righteousness.
> On Christ the solid rock I stand,
> all other ground is sinking sand.

What is the source of our hope? Hope is rooted in God's faithfulness. If it weren't for that, we would find ourselves perpetually on shaky ground. The main reason we have hope is that God is committed to us, and he can be trusted to work in all of life to bring wholeness, healing, and ultimate victory.

Paul says, "Therefore, since we have been justified through faith, we have peace with God . . . and we rejoice in the hope of the glory of God" (Rom. 5:1,2, NIV). In other words, because God believes in us, we are rooted in hope.

The Circle of Hope

In Scripture Paul gives us a "circle of hope." He begins by reminding us that we can have joy in the midst of our suffering "because we know that suffering produces perseverance" (Rom. 5:3).

The Bible is always realistic. There is a certain acceptance of the fact that it is usual and even expected that we will suffer. Paul links our experience of joy and suffering. Isn't it a bit ironic that they appear to go together?

In his book *How Can It Be All Right, When Everything Is All Wrong?*, Lewis Smedes writes about the link between joy and suffering. "You and I were created for joy, and if we miss it, we miss the reason for our existence. . . . If our joy is honest joy, it must somehow be congruous with human tragedy. This is the test of joy's integrity: Is it compatible with pain? . . . Only the heart that hurts has a right to joy."

Even so, we act surprised when we go through difficult times. We can't believe it when something bad happens. God certainly isn't surprised. In fact, the early Christians went through so much suffering that they began to see with their twenty-twenty hindsight that God had actually brought good out of the pain.

Some of us probably feel that we would have earned a Ph.D. in suffering if one were awarded. Some people are experts when it comes to trusting God in the midst of suffering and discovering joy along the way. Have you ever taken a stress test? These tests give us points for the various activities we are engaged in.

Recently I took the test and went off the scale because I was leaving a job, starting a new position, moving with my family to another state, and leading a tour group to the Greek Islands in the midst of the move. If the stress didn't eventually get me, I knew my wife and son were thinking seriously about killing me.

All of us from time to time find ourselves up to our ears in stressful situations, and it is very difficult to come through to the other side. I received a letter from a couple who have had their faith tested by the stress of constant change and challenges.

"Changes!" they write. "In four years we have been adapting to a new home, going through an extended illness with a terminally ill grandchild—trying to recover emotionally from that and her subsequent death. We've faced my husband's angina attack and a heart attack following bypass surgery, as well as a cancer diagnosis. Which brings us to now: selling our home and relocating to another part of the country.

"Each change has put us in a position to wait and accept the challenges as they come. We are grateful for the reminders of God's faithfulness. It helps us to look forward to what the Lord has in store for us next—not to have dread or worry about it."

The letter closes with these words from Romans 15:13, "May the God of *hope* fill you with all joy and peace!" This is a powerful reminder that pain, joy, and hope are all very much a part of our lives.

Suffering produces perseverance. What is perseverance? It is patience, constancy, and staying power. In Scripture there is a powerful link between the experience of pain and patience. Remember the words of James, "Consider it pure joy, whenever you face trials of many kinds, because you know that the testing of your faith develops perseverance. Perseverance must finish its work so that you may be mature and complete, not lacking anything" (James 1:2–4, NIV).

Still, I don't know anyone who likes to wait. Perhaps a contemporary definition of hell is being put on hold and forced to listen to inane background music for eternity. If that won't turn our hearts to Jesus, I don't know what will.

One of the reasons it is so difficult for us to wait is that we have strong compulsions to take charge and make something happen. It is important to recognize that humility and hope go hand in hand when we are in a time of waiting. The kind of perseverance that Scripture is calling us to is only possible because of hope. It is hope that reminds us that God is on our side. Thus we don't wait forever and we don't wait in vain.

Perseverance produces character. Author Gail Sheehy describes character as the "enduring marks left by life that set a person apart as an individual." The very things that we have endured, experienced, and overcome later become the marks of our identity. To be a person of character means that we are authentic people engraved with the unique marks of our life.

Another aspect of character is the mark we bear that is our identification with Jesus Christ. Our character reflects the fact that we belong to him. We no longer live for ourselves. All that we are, have been, and will be is offered to Christ for his purpose and use. He puts his mark on us. With a certification that we belong to him, our future is secure in his loving care. And all his power and resources are released to enable us to fulfill everything that he calls us to do.

Character produces hope. With hope the circle is complete. We have a real faith for real life. But it doesn't end there. We become the bearers of hope to people like us who are waiting to hear the reason for the hope we have within us.

During the past several years, it has been my privilege to co-host the radio program "Everyday People" with my good friend

Randy Rowland. Last summer we spent an afternoon with a remarkable young man named Tony Melendez. You may remember
seeing him play guitar for the pope on television a few years ago.

Tony immigrated from Nicaragua and grew up in a barrio of
East L.A. His lifelong dream was to be a priest in the church he
loved and to care for people in a small parish. After years of study,
his application was refused. Because Tony was born with no
arms, the Vatican ruled him ineligible for service.

Tony returned to Los Angeles, taught himself to play guitar
with his feet, and supported himself as a street musician sitting
on the sidewalk playing hymns for bystanders. It was there that
he was discovered and invited to play and sing for the pope on his
recent visit to our country.

While I watched his performance on television, I was struck
by the spontaneous response of the crowd, and the pope who
made his way past the barricades to reach out and hold Tony
while the whole world looked on.

In his book, *A Gift of Hope*, Tony shares, "After the concert
I walked backstage through the waiting crowd of old friends and
new. . . . At the back of the crowd I saw a badly deformed young
woman in a wheelchair. Her arms and legs were twisted, but she
smiled and tried to wave as I passed. I kept walking toward the
exit; then I stopped, turned around, and walked back in her direction. When she saw me standing beside her, her eyes filled
with tears. She reached her hand out toward me and struggled to
speak. 'Tony,' she said, 'because of you, we all have hope!'"

Perhaps hope is so fragile and fleeting because we recoil and
back away in fear at every opportunity to face life squarely with
the eyes of faith. Wanting to avoid suffering, we settle for shallow, sterile lives. We pick the path of least resistance, rather than
choosing the rocky road of patient perseverance. We gladly settle
for personality and lifestyle rather than character. And we take
wishful thinking over authentic hope.

Tony's experience reminds us that hope is as contagious as it is durable. Perhaps those who discover hope while facing the harsh realities of life also uncover a grace that is more than enough to meet our needs.

CHAPTER EIGHT

Grace and Love

Beloved, let us love one another; for love is of God, and he who loves is born of God and knows God.

1 JOHN 4:7

One word frees us of all the weight and pain of life. And that word is love.

SOPHOCLES

WHEN it comes to love, there are no easy answers. With matters of the heart I find no fixed guidelines to regulate my response or assure success in my relationships. I don't always know how to act loving with the people that matter the most in my life. Sometimes mixed motives and hidden agendas cloud the things that appear to be loving. There are certainly dangers lurking below the surface in every relationship.

Although books and films about love abound, I'm convinced that there are no experts who have it all together in this important area. When it comes to love, we are all novices. In spite of this, there is no end to the sharing of wisdom and advice about love.

One down-to-earth philosopher said, "Love is blind, but marriage is a real eye-opener."

Although it's easy to romanticize love, most of us know the pain and difficulty that accompany close personal relations. After years of marriage and marriage counseling, I still struggle to know and understand Eileen, who remains in many ways a mystery to me. I often miss the clues to her unmet needs and the longing of her heart. At the same time I wonder if my own silent cries will go unheeded.

We spend great amounts of time talking, sharing, fighting, playing, and growing, and we expect our relationships to be easy. If they are not trouble-free, we fear that there is something wrong with us or the other person.

Misconceptions About Love

Perhaps the most pressing need in our lives, our relationships, and our world is to discover the gift of authentic love. But all of us carry a certain amount of baggage when it comes to love. Ideas, expectations, experiences (both good and bad), hopes, and fears all influence how we will respond in our relationships. In order to discover the love that God in his grace gives to us, it is important to set aside some of the misconceptions or myths about love that confuse and ultimately derail us.

Our perspectives about love have been shaded and influenced by trends in culture and media to such an extent that we may need to rediscover what is real and what is not. We have allowed literature, music, and media to influence and even shape some of our views about love to the point where we no longer know the difference between reality and what is fantasy.

If we are to have real-life faith, we must allow God's word to impact our lives, to refine and even redefine how we live. This is particularly true when it comes to love. Look at the following scriptures and see what they are telling us about this strange and wonderful thing called love.

"For God so loved the world that he gave his only Son, that whoever believes in him should not perish but have eternal life. For God sent the Son into the world, not to condemn the world, but that the world might be saved through him"(John 3:16, 17).

"God sent his only Son into the world, so that we may live through him. In this is love, not that we loved God but that He loved us and sent his Son to be the sacrifice for our sins" (I John 4:9, 10).

What Is Love?

Love is the active expression of grace. It is grace in action. Love is an action verb, not a fuzzy, warm feeling. Love is an act of will, not an emotional mood. Love is a commitment to nurture, strengthen, and build up others, not a sentimental journey into Fantasyland.

If we are to separate fantasy from reality, we must understand some basic facts about love.

Love is God's idea. "We love, because He first loved us" (I John 4:19). Our God is not an "absentee landlord" who set the world spinning and then sits apart like a giant gas cloud waiting for us to figure it all out. Scripture is clear that our relationships with God and each other are possible because he loves first. Because he loves us, we are set free to reach out in love to those around us.

Love can be more difficult to accept than to give. In his book *Let God Love You,* Lloyd John Ogilvie made the radical discovery that our problem is not that we have to love God more but that we must find a way to let his love permeate our lives.

For some reason, I want to be the lover and do the giving. I want to appear strong, responsive, and in control. But too often I don't know how to relax and receive the gift of love that God longs to give me. While it may be more blessed to give than to receive, it still remains more difficult to admit we are needy even though we long for assurances that we are truly and unreservedly loved.

Love hurts. Some of us have learned that by avoiding love and intimacy we also can avoid some of the pain that accompanies it. When I read the words from Ezekiel 11:19, "I will remove from them their heart of stone, and give them a heart of flesh" (NIV), I am tempted to question God's wisdom.

Wouldn't you rather have a heart of stone? After all, a heart of stone doesn't break. With a heart of stone, we never have to make ourselves vulnerable. When we are let down or disappointed by others, it wouldn't matter. Who cares if we fail or hurt the ones we love? We have a heart of stone.

But God is in the heart transplant business. And the new heart he gives us is tender. It is vulnerable and it can be broken. "If you love the world long enough," says Bruce Larson, "your heart will eventually be broken."

Perhaps heartbreak is the price of love. Perhaps it is what makes love so powerful, so meaningful, and so costly. Perhaps only those who have had their hearts broken can understand the depth of God's love for each one of us. We also need to know that there is healing for our broken hearts because we belong to God.

Love means we belong. The reality of love is that we belong to God and to each other. This twofold reality is part of our covenant relationship described in the Old Testament. Then "they shall be my people and I will be their God" (Ezek. 11:20). We are not just a bunch of individuals trying to make it as best we can. We are connected in a very real and powerful way by the love of God.

In spite of this fact of life, I still don't feel as if I belong. Most of my own life has been spent struggling against the insecurity of not fitting in, of not belonging. As a teenager, I "went forward" to accept Christ into my life at least fifty or sixty times. Each time a guest speaker or evangelist invited us to be saved, I was reminded of my feeling that I had not done enough to finally belong in the inner circle of the church. So I kept trying to get it right, hoping that eventually I would know without a doubt that I was where I belonged.

This sense of not belonging followed me to school as well. I think the most painful hour of the day for me in high school was the lunch hour. It only took about eight minutes to finish an average brown-bag lunch, which left fifty-two minutes to stand around and pretend that I had friends and that I belonged.

Fortunately I worked out a system that helped me survive those lonely years. It was a simple yet brilliant scam! I found a group of kids that seemed to be everything I wanted in my life. Then I stood on the outer edge of their circle for the entire lunch hour. Though I never actually spoke with them, I would occasionally glance in their direction or chuckle to myself about something they said or did.

They knew I wasn't a part of the group, and I certainly knew I did not belong. But on the outside chance that some other students walked by, they might see me standing near the group and assume that I was part of the "in" crowd.

I carried that same relational insecurity into my later life. I was afraid to love or to let others get close to me. As a pastor, I found myself standing near the circle of fellowship, but I was always a bit removed. Maybe I was afraid that if people were close to me, they would find out that I'm not as loving as I should be or not as sensitive, spiritual, or smart as I could be. Perhaps I would be found out, and then I wouldn't be loved any more.

My own fear kept me from knowing the love I desired. But I was surprised by love. I found that in an incredible act of grace, God had drawn his circle large enough to include even me. In the process, I discover that I am loved regardless and that I belong.

CHAPTER NINE

Grace and Power

Nearly all men can stand adversity, but if you want to test a man's character, give him power.
ABRAHAM LINCOLN

Not by might, nor by power, but by my Spirit, says the Lord of hosts.
ZECHARIAH 4:6

A friend once said to me, "If you aren't even aware of your own power, how are you ever going to use it to build up instead of tearing people down?" I didn't want to hear this, as I looked out over my omelette in the little cafe. I had been telling my friend during breakfast that I felt powerless in so many situations. I had resorted to lashing out when I felt angry and becoming defensive when I felt as if I were attacked. Obviously these reactions weren't getting great results, and I knew I had to try something new.

My friend's suggestion that I wasn't aware of my own power began to make sense to me. I realized that when I blow up in anger or hurt, it is at least partially because I feel powerless to face the challenge in a healthy way. I need to discover the relationship between grace and power.

The Nature of Power

There is something unsettling about power. Have you noticed that we often feel that it is something only other people possess? As my friend reminded me, I am not very aware of my own power, though I'm certainly aware of other people's power. In spite of my best efforts to empower others and not be seen as a "power broker," I still find myself chasing after it. I can be very creative in my pursuit of power, or at least the appearance of power.

A recent headline caught my attention and drew me to one of our newest sporting events called power golf. "Forget the polyester; the Blasters Tourney is for real men." The new national pro tour of the World Power Golf Association is under way. Players call themselves "blasters," and their goal is simply to hit the ball as far as they possibly can. Power golf involves no finesse and no fine-tuned skills—just pure power. It may just catch on.

Is there anything in life that is more desired, feared, helpful, or debilitating than power? We still spend a lot of energy in our quest for power. As Emerson realized, "Life is a search after power." Statesman Stuart Udall, recognizing that power is often misused, said, "We have, I fear, confused power with greatness."

There is no doubt that power has been and continues to be used destructively, rather than redemptively. Power struggles invade our relationships, setting us apart from each other personally, professionally, and sometimes spiritually. We are tempted to play power games and manipulate those around us for our own purposes. We often assert our will against those we love. This drives them away from us and eventually destroys the intimacy we crave.

Whether we possess great power or search for more power, we need to come to grips with power in our own lives and relationships so we can experience the fullness of God's power in us and use it in fresh healing ways.

We can learn a lot about power from Scripture. The Old Testament prophet Isaiah reminded us that power is God's gift to us. "He gives power to the faint, and to him who has no might he increases strength" (Isa. 40:29).

Jesus said to his followers, "All power in heaven and on earth has been given to me. Go therefore and make disciples of all nations. . . ." (Matt. 28:18).

The Book of Acts begins with Jesus' disciples asking about the establishment of a political kingdom on earth. In other words, they wanted to know when they would have power, political strength, and influence. He responds by directing their attention away from political power and toward a spiritual power. He promises to his disciples, "But you shall receive power when the Holy Spirit has come upon you; and you shall be my witnesses . . ." (Acts 1:8).

The power that Jesus promised was not a limited, manipulating, political exercise. Rather it was an explosive, all-consuming spiritual power. The Bible goes on to show how the Church was released for powerful ministry and witness as Jesus' followers experienced the unleashed power of the Holy Spirit.

Power as a gift. One of the key impressions from Scripture about power is that it is not something to be seized, hoarded, or developed. Rather it is something that is given to us. We receive power for specific purposes.

Some people have the mistaken idea that they can parlay spiritual power to their own ends or try to build up their spiritual power. Almost like workouts in the athletic club, they participate in aerobic Bible study, marathon ministries, and low-impact prayer exercises. They try to produce in themselves and sometimes in others the appearance of spiritual strength and vitality.

Of course they are bound to fail because spiritual power cannot be pumped up inside us. It only comes as a gift from God to release us as his witnesses in this world.

Power in community. Power is not only given by the Holy Spirit; it is experienced in community. The Acts of the Apostles tells us, "When the day of Pentecost had come, they were all together in one place. And suddenly a sound came from heaven like a rush of a mighty wind, and it filled all the house where they were sitting" (Acts 2:1, 2). Following Pentecost, Luke tells us, "Many wonders and signs were done through the apostles. And all who believed were together and had all things in common . . . and the Lord added to their number day by day those who were being saved" (Acts 2:43–44, 47).

Why is the power of the Holy Spirit specifically linked to the nurturing fellowship of the community of faith? Perhaps it is because it is so easy to distort power and use it for our own purposes. There is an accountability that keeps us from acting stupid or losing our perspective when we are in committed relationships with others.

Problems tend to develop when we think we don't need others and we strike out on our own. When we feel a little bit of power, we lack the accountability to keep a clear focus and we begin to stray. We use power for our own purposes rather than the purpose for which God called us.

Who needs people to pry into our personal lives, share vulnerably, and make commitments to and with us? Who needs people to say, "What happens to you matters to me"? Who needs people to know us intimately and love us anyway? Who needs people to forgive us when we embarrass ourselves and stand by us so we can grow as men and women of faith? Who needs it? We all do! We all need it because that is the only way to be healthy. It is the way to experience the power of God at work in us and through us.

Power in ministry. The power of God is released in us as we engage in ministry. This raises questions in our minds such as, What is effective ministry? How can I be a minister? How will I know when God wants to use me to help someone? These are all valid questions, and the answers to them are very practical. One of the reasons many of our churches are so pathetic is that they have forgotten that the word *minister* is a verb and not a noun. It is something we do, not something we study or analyze.

Ministry happens when we are interruptible. Acts 3 provides a marvelous glimpse at the anatomy of ministry. "Seeing Peter and John about to go into the Temple, [a lame man] asked for alms" (Acts 3:3). When Peter and John were on their way to the temple in the course of their regular routine, they saw interruption as an opportunity to extend the power of God, not as a drain on their precious limited energy and attention.

I had lunch recently with a friend who works in a fast-paced, rapidly changing industry. She mentioned that the pressures of her work push her to see inconvenience as bad and convenience as good. She says, "When I find myself inconvenienced, I put up barriers and miss out on the good thing that God might want to do in that frustrating moment."

This rings true for me as well. The more pressure I feel in my life, the more I want to streamline everything and make myself practically inaccessible. When I'm in this mindset, I pull back from any interruption as if it were the plague. I know I may be missing out on interesting life experiences, but I still turn away perhaps because I suspect I won't have the power to respond appropriately in the situation.

It is often easier to talk about inconvenience and interruptions than it is to experience them ourselves. One Sunday last year I entered the church where I was scheduled to preach and I discovered that there was a power failure. The sanctuary was in complete darkness without spotlights, heat, or a sound system. Furthermore, there were over 3,500 worshippers scheduled to arrive that morning expecting church as usual.

We scrambled frantically, trying to keep our sense of humor while digging around for old wedding candles and flashlights. The first worship service was progressing reasonably well when, precisely at the point of the sermon where I mentioned that God wants us to be interruptible, a clamor erupted in the first row of the darkened sanctuary.

An obviously drunk streetperson had awakened from his stupor and, seeing the crowd that had gathered, rose to his feet to begin what I assumed to be his own variation of the sermon. Though the sanctuary was numbingly cold, I was sweating profusely. I had just said that God wants us to be interruptible, and I was watching a drama unfold that threatened to derail the whole worship service.

Finally, in desperation, I stopped the man and told him that he could not interrupt the service and that he should finish his talk out on the sidewalk. At that point he suddenly turned and ran out of the sanctuary, leaving me to salvage what was left of the sermon on being interruptible.

Setting my notes aside, I shared with the congregation that not all interruptions are from God. Furthermore, it is not always easy to know when to set aside our agenda for the sake of the immediate distraction and when to set aside the interference. There are no simple guidelines; we make our decisions in faith and trust God to redeem the best and worst moments in our day.

After the service, many people commented on how clever I was to bring in an actor and stage the interruption to dramatize the sermon. Some even thought that the special effects of keeping off the lights enhanced the worship service. The worship department thought that perhaps we should try more theatrical stunts like this in the future. I kept telling them it was real, but no one seemed to believe me.

Ministry happens when we take people seriously. "Peter directed his gaze at him, with John, and said, 'Look at us' " (Acts 3:4). How do you feel when someone takes you seriously? What goes through your mind when you sense that you are merely being tolerated? One of the greatest gifts we can give to one another is the gift of our attention.

As I travel throughout the country speaking in churches and conferences, I am glad to find in virtually every gathering a few men and women who practice the ministry of taking people seriously. Some have been through extensive training, and others rely on natural instincts. But they have all found creative ways to come alongside others who are going through difficult or painful times in order to be caring, tuned-in friends. They tell me that it is often hard work to listen without judging and to ask questions that enable others to open up rather than shut down. It can be hard work to walk alongside people to help them grow and heal. I know it takes time, energy, and effort, so I salute these modern heroes who have discovered a secret of authentic ministry.

Sadly, it is a rare and valued treasure to have people in our lives who take us seriously. They will not offer simple answers to our questions or dismiss us with a cliche or Bible verse but will honor us by focusing their attention and allowing God to bring healing in his time.

Of course, the issue is not how we can get these people to listen to us. Rather it is how we can become like them and be caring friends to the ones around us who need us.

Peter and John focused on the person, took him seriously, looked beyond the surface to see the need, and reached out and lifted him up. God brought the healing.

Power in Witness. Jesus promised that when the Holy Spirit comes, his disciples will have power and be his witnesses. The power of God is always released for a purpose. It is not for personal glory or to be used as an end in itself. Rather it always points back to Jesus Christ. It is a witness to his life, love, grace, and power.

Sometimes we are tempted to separate ministry from witness. We hold back from telling our story of coming into a relationship with Christ. Instead we settle for a "good deeds" type of behavior hoping it makes its own silent witness. Our witness can become distant and separated from our relationships and ministry. We forget that the power is given so that we may be witnesses.

Peter used the occasion of healing not as an end in itself but as an opportunity to explain that it is Jesus who is behind everything. The rulers became annoyed because the disciples kept talking about Jesus, so they arrested them and held a trial. But we cannot refute the simple facts and the power of their witness.

"But when they saw their boldness and perceived that they were uneducated, common people, they wondered; and they recognized that they had been with Jesus. And seeing the man that had been healed standing beside them, they had nothing to say in opposition" (Acts 4:13, 14).

My friend was right; I wasn't aware of my own power. I settled for posturing and positioning myself to appear more powerful than I felt, but I didn't believe that God's power was really available for me. I need gentle reminders from those around me that I don't have to manipulate or engage in power games. Instead I can accept the power that comes from simply sharing the ongoing struggles and victories that come while I follow Jesus. I'm beginning to discover that there is power when I allow divine appointment to interrupt my precious schedule. There is power when I'm willing to look people in the eye and see beyond the surface so I can be involved in other's lives. Then I realize that God is at work in me with grace and power.

CHAPTER TEN

Grace and Vision

Where there is no vision, the people perish.
PROVERBS 29:18

I was a second-class Boy Scout and proud of it! The rank of second class was bestowed on me with great ceremonial dignity, and I was quite relieved to have risen in the ranks beyond my former position as a tenderfoot scout. However, in order to fulfill the rigorous demands of second-classhood, I had to prove my scouting abilities in the wilds of Camp Cuyamacka.

Three whole days at scout camp was a challenge that I was prepared to undertake. I had my backpack filled with needed equipment like cans of Spam, my compass, my mess kit, and even the amazing all-purpose scouting knife. I had heard all about digging latrines, cooking on an open fire, and protecting myself against bear attacks (don't put the leftover Spam under your pillow).

My only concern, and it was a very small one, was what to do if I got lost. I imagined myself wandering in the woods for days, living on carefully rationed daily allowances of Spam and, of course, any wild animals I might harvest with my scout knife. Jay Schwartz, an older, experienced Eagle Scout, noticed that I was

looking less than totally confident as we set up our pup tents, and
he finally asked me what was bothering me.

"How will I know if I'm lost?" I asked. "I might go off exploring and not even realize that I am lost."

Jay laughed and said, "Just remember you are never lost as
long as you remember where you are going. You may not see
very far in front of you, and you may not know exactly where you
are, but if you remember where you are going, you are not lost."

At various times in my life I have felt confused, disoriented,
and even unclear about the steps before me. But I think my old
scout buddy was right. Vision is the gift of remembering where
we are going.

Vision, spiritually speaking, is a vital and essential part of our
lives together as followers of Jesus Christ. It is important to keep
in mind where we are going so we don't become disoriented or
diverted onto side trails that get us off course. I'm grateful for
the vision that has been fostered among Christians throughout
the world. Our vision is not a laser-beam single-mindedness; it is
more like bifocal lenses on a pair of eyeglasses. Our vision is
clearer when we maintain a two-part focus that involves attention
to our inner spiritual growth and a clear focus on human needs
around us. We keep our eyes on Jesus Christ, knowing that it is in
relationship with him that our salvation and spiritual health lies.
We also keep our eyes on the needs of people, staying deeply involved in our community and in the world.

It is not easy to maintain this balance of perspective. There
are always those who would throw sand in our eyes to promote a
self-indulgent false spirituality. They would challenge us to pull
away from the world so that the "stink" doesn't get on us.

These people may practice spiritual exercises like prayer, worship, and Bible study, but it is always at a distance from the real
world. Their lack of awareness of people outside the circle leads to
indifference. This indifference leads to fear, and the fear leads to

resentment. They often hold back from taking risks in life so they can protect and preserve the image they want to portray.

On the other hand, there are also those who divert us from our focus on personal spiritual growth. Assuming that political change and community involvement will lead to fulfillment, these people focus on the outside world and neglect the deeper longings of our personal lives.

Vision gives us the courage to move beyond simplistic categories and challenges us to live with balance. We encourage personal spiritual growth through Bible study, prayer, discipleship, and covenant groups. But we also live with one foot in the world. Our lives must be lived every day in the streets, neighborhoods, offices, and schools of our community and beyond.

For me there is a built-in tension between my personal needs and my sensitivity to the needs of others. There seems to be an ebb and flow in the amount of emotional energy I can invest in either myself or others. If I spend too much time and energy focusing on those around me, I begin to feel dry inside, and the result is inevitable brittleness. I become short-tempered, demanding, and (according to my wife) I can turn into Mr. Insensitive. Likewise, when I find myself excessively looking inward, I can become aloof, guarded, and unwilling to take risks or step out of my comfort zone.

Finding the balance for me is a continuing experiment. Just when I think I have it right, something or someone enters my sight line, and once again my vision is out of focus.

One of my favorite stories involves the great medical missionary David Livingstone who was photographed standing with his hand shielding his eyes as he surveyed the vast expanse of African landscape that surrounded him.

A reporter commented on how striking the picture was and wondered what was going through the great doctor's mind at the moment the picture was taken. "Were you by any chance considering the words of our Lord when he said, 'The fields are ripe unto harvest, Behold the harvest is plentiful, but the laborers are few'?"

Dr. Livingstone thought for a minute and said, "No, I was telling the photographer that I was tired and that I had it up to here with all the problems and hassles of this ministry. I guess that was the moment he took my picture."

Sometimes when we find ourselves in the thick of it, involved in people's lives, learning, growing, and caring, it is easy to lose perspective. We need continual reminders of who God is, who we are, and how we can serve him in our world so we can maintain a sense of confidence and joy while we stay focused on the vision before us.

Matthew 14 provides some important lessons to help us balance our vision. It is a time of transition for Jesus and his disciples. Jesus has experienced rejection in his hometown. His cousin, John the Baptist, has been beheaded, and an era of prophetic and dramatic ministry has ended.

We find Jesus filled with compassion for crowds who have followed him as he sets to work ministering to their particular needs. At the end of the day, the disciples let him know that it is time to close up shop. "This is a lonely place, and the day is now over; send the crowds away to go into the villages and buy food for themselves." But Jesus said, "They need not go away; you give them something to eat" (Matt. 14:15, 16).

I am beginning to think that if we are doing it right, there will always be a built-in tension between the apparent needs around us that cry out to be met and our ability to meet the needs with the limited resources we have. There will never be enough food, time, energy, creativity, money, buildings, parking, medicine, counselors, Bibles, or whatever, to completely satisfy the diverse demands that are placed before us on a daily basis.

Thus the issue is not whether we can be sure we have enough to accomplish the task, for that is impossible, but whether we will bring what we have and present it to the Lord for his use. The disciples said, "We have only five loaves here and two fish." And he said, "Bring them here to me"(Matt. 14:17, 18). Jesus then took the bread and the fish, gave thanks, broke the bread, and gave it to the disciples instructing them to give it to the people gathered.

You know the rest of the story. The disciples kept breaking the bread and serving the people, and there was plenty for everyone, enough to meet every hunger, with some left over. This Scripture doesn't go into technical detail about how this happened, but I imagine that the disciples were perpetually on the brink of running out of food as they were feeding the crowds.

I believe that they were always one serving away from running out of food. That day, every man, woman, and child in the crowd required a miracle in order to be fed. And in the same way, as we live out our faith with compassion and care, we are very aware that we are one step away from not having what it takes to meet the needs all around us. We have to rely on God alone to provide miraculously or we are in big trouble.

Look what follows in the Scripture passage. The disciples are out in their boat, still marveling at the miracle in which they were involved. They see Jesus walking toward them on the water, and they become frightened. Peter, still giddy from the feeding, gets out of the boat at Christ's invitation and walks out on the water to meet his master.

But something goes wrong. "But when he saw the wind, he was afraid, and beginning to sink, he cried out, 'Lord save me'" (Matt. 14:30).

Have you ever felt like you were in over your head? Perhaps like Peter, you were a little zealous and found yourself unable to finish what you believed God called you to do? It's easy in times like this to feel distracted, confused, fearful, and even discouraged. When we take our eyes off Jesus and begin to focus on the wind—the impending problems—we start to sink.

Notice that Peter didn't see the waves or the deep churning sea, but he saw the wind. Have you ever seen the wind? We cannot actually see it; we can only see the effects of it. Perhaps Peter was afraid of what may happen as a result of the wind, the unknown, the *what-ifs*. The wind is uncontrollable; it is a force that he has no power to control.

What is the wind in your life? The unseen, uncontrollable forces that paralyze you with fear. The words that fill your heart with dread and stifle your creativity. The what-ifs or if-onlys in your life that remind you that you don't have what it takes to be victorious. What are some things that cloud your thoughts with worry and remind you that you are in way over your head? What causes you to take your eyes off of Jesus and start to sink?

One of the songs that I learned as a child in Sunday school is a reminder of the need to sharpen our spiritual vision. "Turn Your Eyes Upon Jesus" was written by Helen Lemmel, a longtime member of the Seattle church where I was a pastor. Helen lived up the street from the church and was often seen making her way into worship with the help of a white cane. Though she was blind physically, she had very sharp spiritual vision and knew where to put her trust.

Where will we put our trust? Will we put it in the wind, the storms, and the unseen forces that swirl around and pressure us? Will we, like the first disciples, trust in the boat and sit safely in its shelter, never stepping out and getting in over our heads, never taking risks or living in such a way that we can't guarantee the results? Or will we keep our eyes on Jesus, trusting him to make good out of the stresses of our lives?

While living in a homeless shelter in Kansas City, Missouri, Rosemary Pritchett was surprised to find an endorsed check for $400 on the sidewalk. She and her three children had been saving bits of money in hope of buying an abandoned house so they could leave the homeless shelter. Rosemary was committed to doing the right thing, so she called Cheryl Wood, the person who had lost the check, and returned it that evening.

When Cheryl heard about the Pritchett's efforts to move into the abandoned house, she wanted to help but she didn't know the extent of the problem. "I asked what her color schemes would be," says Wood. "It just shows how naive I was." When she dropped by to see the house, she was shocked to find windows boarded up and the children inside trying to tear out broken walls with small hand tools.

Determined to make a difference, Cheryl soon recruited nearly seventy volunteers from her church, including a contractor and a decorator. Soon the house was restored and the Pritchett family moved from the shelter into their new home.

Grace and vision go hand in hand. When asked if she ever considered not returning the lost check, Rosemary said, "Not for a tiny moment did I think of cashing the check. . . . I know that if I keep my eyes on the Lord, then everything will fall into place."

She realized the secret of grace and vision: Keep your eyes on Jesus, and stay tuned in to the needs and cares of people all around us. With this bifocal outlook, I remember where I'm going and I am never really lost.

PART III

Grace to Encourage

CHAPTER ELEVEN

Raising the Standards: Legalism

Law is a bottomless pit.
JOHN ARBUTHNOT

*W*HILE driving into the tiny town of Asti in the wine-growing region of California, I noticed an old billboard welcoming travelers to the rustic town. The sign read, "Welcome to Asti. We've upped our standards, so up yours."

Later as I thought about the welcome sign, I realized that although the message is funny and quite clever, it also illustrates the tension we have between the desire to raise our standards and the tendency to look down on others who don't measure up to them.

Like most heresies, legalism is a good thing gone wrong. We all live somewhat in accordance with laws; they help us regulate our behavior and provide consistency of sorts in our social exchanges. But too much of a good thing can become detrimental.

Despite my good intentions, I still find myself inching toward the pit of legalism time and again. Sometimes it's a subtle flinching in my stomach when someone doesn't perform according to my preconceived ideas. Other times I may hear myself blasting out in a critical diatribe against those who don't please me. Usually I'm able to justify my attitude by demonstrating how I am clearly right even though I neglect the equally obvious fact that I am being legalistic and unloving.

Jesus struggled against the enforcers and interpreters of the law throughout his ministry. The Apostle Paul writing in Philippians calls them dogs and warns other Christians to beware of those who would set up arbitrary standards for our faith.

Legalism may be one of the most subtle yet destructive heresies that threatens our faith, destroys our freedom, and smothers our joy. Why is it so dangerous?

It is dangerous because it takes our eyes off Jesus as the source of our life and faith and focuses attention on actions, behaviors, and external standards. What begins innocently as the raising of standards ends up as a stumbling block to our faith.

Today there are those who would add on to the simple truth of the gospel, raise the standards, and in effect say, "Jesus is not enough. You must also add. . . ." We may start to believe that faith in Jesus is all right as far as it goes, but find that we need something more tangible. We want something else to hold on to. How does this happen? Anytime we take a behavior or a response and make it a precondition to following Christ or a mark of being a real Christian, we are guilty of the sin of legalism.

There are many modern-day legalists in the church today. Some judge others by spiritual criteria and try to establish measurable standards of faithfulness. For instance, I have some charismatic friends who sincerely believe that if you don't speak in tongues, what they call the Baptism of the Spirit, you are not really a Christian. Others try to make lifestyle issues the criterion for judging the faithful.

A while ago, Randy Rowland and I were recording one of our "Everyday People" radio programs with our friend Tony Campolo.

We love interviewing Tony because he gets very passionate and outspoken about issues and concerns in our world. During the interview Tony was his usual exuberant self, challenging the complacency and comfort of most middle-American Christians who he thinks are not diligent enough in living a simple lifestyle and giving more money to help the poor.

Suddenly he hit close to home when he said, "You cannot be a Christian and drive a BMW." I almost came out of my chair. I used to have a BMW, and at the time I was driving a British sports car. Randy smugly smiled at me because he drives a Mercedes and therefore still qualifies as a good Christian.

We argued back and forth in a sometimes not-so-good-natured debate. I finally told Tony that he represents the new breed of pharisee and legalist for this generation. He told me I was a self-indulgent yuppie scum. Furthermore, I reminded him that Judas must have been his patron saint. For it was Judas of all the disciples who was upset at Jesus for not giving more to missions and helping more with the poor. Tony encouraged me to get serious about my faith and start reading the Bible instead of *Motor Trend* magazine. As we broke for a commercial, Randy tried to pull us together by saying that we are not really that far apart in our opinions. To which Tony and I both yelled, "Yes, we are!"

After the show we had a good laugh together and agreed that it's easy to set up rules and arguments to justify our positions. We also agreed that how we live and the choices we make have an impact on those around us.

Tony reminded me that I need to look at the world with fresh eyes and encourage others to do the same so we can see the needs around us. This will enable me to ask God what he wants to happen in me or through me in these situations. I reminded him that at the same time we dare not presume or dictate the response other people should make once they have been confronted with the needs. As soon as we do, we assume the place of God by establishing standards and judging others according to our priorities and perspectives.

In the process we turn away from a living, vital relationship with the person Jesus Christ and start to become religious. Jesus did not come to earth two thousand years ago to live among us, die on the cross, and rise from the dead so that we can be more religious. His death loosened the grip of religion forever.

Religion with its laws and standards represents some of our best efforts to earn our way to heaven. It supposes that we are separated from God and only able to reach up by our own efforts and good works. It is as if God is a dysfunctional parent figure whose message to us is "I will only love you if . . . (you are perfect, holy, good, nice, successful, quiet, or whatever)."

I was caught up in the game of trying to be religious, and before too long I found myself unwittingly trying to satisfy a god that seemed distant and aloof. I tried hard to overcome every obstacle and setback with persistence and hard work, and all the while I had a gnawing suspicion that I was not yet good enough.

Of course, along the way it became necessary to present myself in the best light so that others wouldn't know that I was not as good as I appeared. One way I found to protect myself was to only show my victories, successes, and strengths. The result of these futile efforts was that when I would act this way, I'd have a tendency to feel either guilty or smug and self-righteous.

I had forgotten that the forgiveness of sin, offered in Jesus' death, is a great equalizer for all people. The good and strong no longer have any advantage over the weak and fallible. We are no longer held back or trapped in the web of guilt and shame.

Neither can we credit ourselves with the personal strength to overcome and emerge victoriously according to our ability. We all stand before God on an equal footing. We are judged not by our goodness or badness but solely on our relationship with Jesus Christ and our trust in him.

This is a relief to some of us, but it makes others a bit uncomfortable. In Matthew 23, Jesus goes straight to the heart of the matter in his confrontation with the legalists of his day. First, he warns them that their priorities are out of order. "Woe to you, scribes and Pharisees, hypocrites! For you tithe mint and dill and cummin, and have neglected the weightier matters of the law, justice and mercy and faith; these you ought to have done, without neglecting the others. You blind guides, straining out a gnat and swallowing a camel!"(Matt. 23:23).

The religious people were faithful to tithe, in fact so faithful that they worked hard to figure out ten percent of the chili powder. But in the process they lost sight of what was most important. Their perspective became skewed.

Doesn't that happen to us when we are so attentive to the letter of the law that we neglect, ignore, or turn our backs on the spirit that was intended? Like the Volunteer Fire Department in Arkansas that drew criticism for letting a house burn down because the owner hadn't paid a twenty-dollar annual fee for fire-fighting service. Because of their inaction, two adjacent furniture shops were destroyed. A resident behind the shops paid the fee while the fire was burning, reported Chief Ronnie Courtney. "After the fire started, they joined," he told reporters. "Once your house is on fire, you can't join, but if you're a neighbor to some property that's on fire, you can join." When the house burned down, firefighters stood by to see that the blaze didn't spread to the homes of people who had paid the twenty-dollar fee.

Looking through the eyes of legalism is like looking through the wrong end of the telescope. Suddenly our world and viewpoint get very small. When we are driven by the law, there is a natural tendency to become enmeshed in minutia. We become unable or unwilling to discern what is important. Even worse, we try to cover up and blame others, often using the law as our means of self-justification.

Homer Simpson, the father on the cartoon show "The Simpsons," is a master at covering up and blaming others. In one episode, when he thought he might be dying from some bad sushi he had eaten, he took his young son Bart aside to share with him some of the most important lessons a father must pass on to his children. "Remember these words, Bart," Homer said. " 'It was like that when I found it.' 'It's not my fault.' 'He did it.' " In other words, lie, cover up, and when all else fails, blame someone else. Too often these are the real lessons that we unwittingly pass on to others.

Jesus doesn't do away with high standards. For example, he doesn't say, "You don't have to tithe." What he does say is that we should pursue justice, mercy, and faith as well as tithe. Let's look at this for a moment. What is the purpose of tithing? It is not a standard that says you have finally measured up. It is a biblical challenge to set aside ten percent of our earnings to demonstrate in a tangible way that we are willing to acknowledge that God is Lord of our finances as well as our spiritual life. In other words, "If he hasn't become Lord of our wallets, he probably isn't Lord of our hearts."

Turning that into a binding law misses the point. We do not tithe in order to prove that we measure up as Christians, and we don't compare our giving with others to see how we are doing. It is not tithing that enables us to stand loved, accepted, and forgiven before God. Rather it is because we stand loved, accepted, and forgiven before God that we are freely motivated to give without compulsion, guilt, or strings.

Then Jesus said, "Woe to you, for you cleanse the outside of the cup and plate, but inside they are full of extortion and rapacity. First cleanse the inside of the cup and plate, that the outside also may be clean" (Matt. 23:25–26).

This warning relates to a preoccupation with ceremonial appearance, rather than an authentic purity. Most of us grew up with the solemn dread, "What will the neighbors say?" hanging over our heads. This concern over appearances haunts us in our adult lives.

Purity in the Bible is related more to who we are than what we do. The word *pure* means "clear all the way through, without flaws or cloudiness." In other words, we are women and men who are the same on the inside as we are on the outside—clear all the way through.

The promise of Scripture is "If we confess our sins, he is faithful and just and will forgive our sins . . . and cleanse us from all unrighteousness" (1 John 1:9). This cleansing doesn't start with the externals. Rather God gets to the core and begins his cleansing, healing work in the deepest recesses of our hearts and minds. He begins to change our motivations and our addictions, our fears and our doubts. He is our Saviour and Lord, not our behavioral therapist.

Along the same lines, Jesus continues, "Woe to you, hypocrites . . . you are like whitewashed tombs, which outwardly appear beautiful, but within they are full of dead men's bones and all uncleanness. So you also outwardly appear righteous to men, but within you are full of hypocrisy and iniquity" (Matt. 23:27, 28).

In an interview in *The Door,* Scott Peck tells about the first time he went to hear the Swiss physician Paul Tournier. Following the lecture there was a time of questions and dialogue, at which point a man stood up and asked, "Dr. Tournier, what do you think about all the hypocrites in the churches of America?" Stumbling over the English words, Tournier apologized and said he did not understand the meaning of the word *hypocrite.* Several people offered definitions. "Phony, pretending to be something that they're not, unauthentic, false." Suddenly the doctor's eyes lit up. "Ah, hypocrites, now I understand. . . . C'est moi! C'est moi. I am the hypocrite."

Health begins when we realize that we are sick. Salvation begins when we sense our own need. Christ takes hold of us when we finally stop trying to make it on our own. We become authentic when we confess, "C'est moi. It is me."

The law is a wonderful thing, for it is God's way of getting our attention. Jesus said, "I don't come to do away with the law, but to fulfill it."

In London we were able to get tickets to see *Les Miserables,* a very passionate play about grace and law. The main character, Jean Valjean, has been imprisoned for years for stealing a piece of bread to feed his starving family. Upon his release from prison he finds shelter at the house of a bishop who feeds him and provides a place to sleep. While his hosts sleep, he steals from the bishop valuable items including the silver goblets that they had drunk from at dinner.

He is arrested and brought back to the bishop so that the stolen goods can be identified. When the bishop sees him captured, he turns and places two silver candelabras into the robber's sack, saying, "In your hurry to leave you must have forgotten that I wanted you to have these as well. . . . Please take them now."

In that moment when grace breaks into the man's life and law is overpowered, Jean Valjean realizes, "My life has been bought back by God. From this day on, I belong to Him."

The jailer, Javier, on the other hand, has committed his entire life to enforcing the letter of the law. Toward the end of the play, he is captured and condemned to die. However, Jean Valjean intercedes and sets him free as an act of grace. Javier, choosing to die rather than accept the free gift of grace, leaps to his death.

Jesus Christ fulfilled the law when he freely died so that we may live. This grace and forgiveness is for every person without exception. There is nothing you can do to get God to love you one bit more than he does right now.

Sometimes I'm tempted to turn away, saying, "I'd rather die than live by grace." But every once in a while I discover the courage to say, "From this day on, I live for him. It is for me that he died. C'est moi!"

CHAPTER TWELVE

Reducing the Standards: License

License they mean when they cry liberty.
JOHN MILTON

*I*T'S no secret that most of us have a deep longing to be free. I hate to feel restricted or held back in any way. My heroes are usually people who fight against constricting regulations in their search for freedom. I identify with Paul Newman's character in *Cool Hand Luke,* who refused to give in to the unfair prison system. When the warden drawls, "What we have here is failure to communicate," I cheer in my heart.

I learned early in life that no matter how bad things were I could always escape in my mind. I became a reader and a day-dreamer. Books took me to different worlds and introduced me to a whole new set of characters. At different times I was intrigued, amused, and even frightened. But when I was really frightened, I could close the book and let my emotions calm down before I plunged back into the story.

Whether our escape is through reading or planning elaborate jailbreaks, we all have in common a pull to break through the bonds we suspect are holding us back. We all want to be free from unreasonable restrictions and have the freedom to decide what is best for us.

It is important to remember that *God cares about our freedom*. Christ came so that we could be free. Paul writes, "For freedom Christ has set us free" (Gal. 5:1).

But for the most part we do not live our lives in the freedom that God intended when he first thought of us. Something has gone terribly wrong. We live lives "of quiet desperation" as Jim Morrison reminded us when he sang for The Doors. We too often feel trapped, held back, and unable to soar or attain the freedom and joy that seems to allude us on a regular basis.

What is freedom? There are a number of definitions. One of my favorites comes from Kris Kristofferson: "Freedom's just another word for nothing left to lose." As long as we cling to our baggage and hold on with all of our strength, we are never really free. It's only when we let go that we become free.

In the Bible, freedom, or liberty, has two components. There is "freedom from" and "freedom for." Paul reminds us in Ephesians 4:17–19 that we are freed *from* having to live in the futility, stupidity, and darkened understanding of those who don't know God. (He is not very subtle, is he?) He goes on to say that we have the freedom from the "old self with its corruption and deceitful desires." We also have freedom *for* putting on the new self created to be like God, with true righteousness and holiness.

We have freedom from lying, stealing, laziness, bitterness, and so on, and we have freedom for kindness, compassion, and forgiveness both for ourselves and others in our lives. In Romans 6, we see that we have freedom from sin ("we are dead to sin") and freedom for "being alive to God in Christ Jesus."

Ironically, some people may find the rigid structure of the law surprisingly freeing. Psychologists tell us that structure reduces anxiety. If that is true, one way to be free from anxiety is to rigidly structure every aspect of our lives so that we know what to expect at any moment, feel a sense of personal control, and therefore live without surprises.

For those of us who live rigid and inflexible lives, freedom will most likely not be a rigidly structured experience. I can identify with the busy executive who lives the fast-paced, frantic life of a corporate environment. For her, life is segmented into neat intervals of time. Her "daytimer" book is her bible, for it keeps her on schedule, reminds her of upcoming responsibilities, and alerts her to variances in her commitments. (Maybe when I die, they should just stick my calender book on my tombstone as the mark of my life, identity, and worth.) We long for a bit of down time. Time without expectations or performance attachments, when we can just make it up as we go along. Freedom means getting away from schedules, appointments, rushing, and pushing. It means asking "What do I want?" instead of "What will be good business?"

We live in the shadow of constant pressure and tension in our lives. Sometimes when we experience stress we get the urge to take control and establish arbitrary standards so we don't have to live by faith. This is the lure of legalism. The other tension is the urge to lower the standards and assume that it doesn't matter how we live because we are forgiven people. This is the heresy of license.

We have seen that many heresies begin with something good, a grain of truth, and then distort it until it becomes false and harmful. This can happen when we distort God's gift of freedom and turn it into license. It is easy to use words like *freedom* or *liberty,* when in fact we mean something else altogether.

John Milton wrote, "License they mean when they cry liberty." At the root of license may be our fear that we can't trust Christ to be adequate for us. We feel drawn to lower the standards in order to get by on our own terms. We ourselves determine what is good or bad. We decide what is the *right* thing to do in any situation, and eventually we set ourselves up as the final authority for our lives. We become like the runner who lowers the hurdles before the race so he can run faster, but who by his action disqualifies himself and loses the race.

The Apostle Paul makes the declaration, "But where sin increased, grace increased all the more" (Rom. 5:20, NIV). This was intended to be a resounding assurance of the overwhelming power of grace in our lives. Paul, however, was a realist. He understood our tendency to twist the truth for our own purposes. So he asks the question and states the obvious answer, "What shall we say then? Shall we go on sinning so that grace may increase? By no means!" (Romans 6:1).

Remember, sin is not just what we do. It is also related to who we are—our character, attitudes, and both the outer acts and inner intentions and secrets of our heart. Sin is missing the mark, falling short of what God meant for us to be. It isn't a popular word, but it is important if we are to discover the freedom to overcome it.

Sin is our choice. There are no helpless victims, nor can we claim, "The devil made me do it!" God has given us the power to choose how we will live and whom we will serve. He has given us the freedom to live victoriously because Christ has broken the power of sin.

"In order to be healthy," writes Frederick Buechner in his book *Wishful Thinking,* "there are certain rules you can break only at your peril. . . . Avoid bottles marked poison, don't jump out of boats unless you can swim, etc. In order to be happy, there are also certain rules you can break only at your peril . . . get rid of hatred and envy, tell the truth, avoid temptations to evil you're not strong enough to resist, don't murder, steal, etc. . . . Both sets of rules . . . describe not the way people feel life ought to be but the way they have found it is." That's just the way life is. But we

do not have to lower ourselves to accommodate a dying world.
Rather we have the freedom and the power to break the mold and
overcome the very evil that would enslave us. Why does Scripture
emphasize this? Because Paul understood that when we lower the
standards for our lives and abdicate our power over sin, we begin a
downward cycle that is self-destructive to the point of death. We
are engaged, according to Scripture, in a battle for our very lives.
Bob Dylan sings:

> Warning signs are flashing by us but we pay no heed.
> Instead of slowin' down, we keep pickin' up speed.
> Disaster's gettin' closer every time we meet,
> Doin' ninety miles an hour down a dead-end street.
>
> You belong to someone else, and I do too.
> It's just as crazy bein' here with you
> As a bad motorcycle with the devil in the seat,
> Doin' ninety miles an hour down a dead-end street

At those times when I am moving along the path to self-
destructive behavior, I'm not always aware of the results of my action. We don't always see the end result of knocking over a single
domino or where our action leads. This was illustrated recently
when I heard about a way that Eskimos kill wolves. I realize that
it is a bit grisly and not very politically correct, yet it offers fresh
insight into the consuming, self-destructive nature of sin.

The hunter begins by repeatedly covering a knife blade with
animal blood and allowing it to freeze until the knife is totally
hidden by the frozen blood. The knife is set into the ground with
the blade pointed up so that the wolf will be lured by the smell of
blood and begin licking the blood-soaked blade.

His hunger for blood causes him to lap the blade and not
notice the slashing of the knife blade against his tongue. Not
knowing that his own blood is mixed with the frozen blood, the
wolf goes on and on until he is found dead in the snow.

When Paul reminds us that "the wages of sin is death," he is not pronouncing sentence as our judge. He is merely presenting us with the facts of life without embellishment. Like Sergeant Joe Friday of "Dragnet," he gives us "Just the facts, Ma'am."

This may come quickly and unexpectedly. It may also come slowly, like the way we die a little inside when we turn our backs on what God intends for us. We find ourselves dying spiritually, we start to dry up inside, and we feel cut off from the joy and fulfillment we seek. Then our relationships start to die. In our marriages, love turns to resentment, which turns to selfish isolation, which leads to a cold stalemate of death. You know what I'm talking about. It has happened to all of us more times than we want to admit.

This may all be true, but it isn't good news. "The wages of sin is death" would be what Bonhoeffer called the *penultimate* or next to last word. God in his mercy will have the last word, and that word is *grace*.

"The wages of sin is death, but the gift of God is eternal life in Jesus Christ our Lord" (Rom. 6:23). Whenever we see the transition word *but*, we can interpret it to mean "ignore everything that went before." It is like the words of a callow lover, "I love you; you're beautiful; I want to spend my whole life with you; *but* I'm not the marrying kind."

If *sin* is the penultimate word, *grace* is the ultimate word. If *death* is the next to last word, *eternal life* is the last word. When we say yes to Jesus Christ and allow him to enter our lives and live within us, the power of sin is broken. We are no longer slaves to its deadly grip. We are free. We are free to live in grace, in power, in peace, and with purpose. We have alternatives.

The first step on the road to life is confession. We must begin to tell the truth about ourselves. "If we confess our sins, he is faithful and just, and will forgive our sins and cleanse us from all unrighteousness" (1 John 1:9).

Our confession can be as simple and authentic as the words of C. S. Lewis who confessed to being a "bundle of self-centered fears, hopes, greeds, jealousies, and self-conceit, all doomed to death." This kind of honesty opens the door to forgiveness and freedom as we discover grace at the point of our greatest need. It also draws us toward each other. I can relate to this type of confession precisely because it is my confession, too. Until I saw his words, I didn't realize how much like C. S. Lewis I am.

Secondly, we open our lives to Jesus Christ. "Behold I stand at the door and knock; if anyone hears my voice and opens the door, I will come in" (Rev. 3:20, KJV). No matter how good or bad our actions have been, Jesus stands at the door wanting to enter our lives and live in and through us. We have only to say yes to enter a personal relationship with the person who will set us free.

Finally, we must let ourselves grow. We need the food of Scripture, the care of a small group, and the challenge of ministry in order to be stretched and renewed. I can only grow if I allow Christ to permeate every aspect of my life. I must get out of his way so he can become the Lord of my work, my play, my problems, and even my victories.

CHAPTER THIRTEEN

Refusing the Standards: Denial

The fish are the last ones to know they are underwater.
ANONYMOUS

I passed a woman on the sidewalk recently who was wearing a T-shirt that caught my attention. It said, "I may not be Cleopatra, but I am the queen of de-nile."

Denial is nothing new, though we tend to think we practice it more than previous generations. Denial comes in several different forms. We deny our emotions such as anger, grief, or anxiety. We deny problems with relationships. The woman or man in an abusive relationship may deny the problem by rationalizing, "It's not that bad; it's all my fault." When a couple divorces, it's not uncommon for the spouse who is left to deny the termination of the marriage. "She will be back; this isn't happening; it's just a misunderstanding; she will come home soon."

Addicts often cover themselves with a cloud of denial saying, "I can stop anytime I want; I don't have a problem," while codependents live in denial and often enable destructive behavior to continue under their unseeing eyes. The odd thing about denial is that while we don't see it in ourselves, it is glaringly obvious to everyone around us.

Today denial may be an overused word, but spiritual denial is as old as the Bible. Throughout the history of God's interaction with humanity, we find people hiding themselves and covering up, refusing to see reality about themselves or about God. This condition may be one of the greatest obstacles to God's rule in our lives and in our world. While legalism is raising the standards to establish arbitrary measures to judge others according to one's performance, and license is lowering the standards to establish ourselves as the determiner of morality, denial is refusing the standards. Denial can be one of the greatest obstacles to healing because it is the refusal to see our need or admit there is a problem.

My wife and I recently observed a man in a restaurant who was committed to having a quiet, romantic candlelight dinner with his companion. Nothing would divert him from his goal. He didn't look up when a distinguished young man in formal tails and a top hat quietly entered the dining room and approached the table next to him. He never flinched when without warning the stranger set up a portable stereo beside the table, removed a violin from a carrying case, and began to serenade the guests at a dinner party nearby. As the talented stranger sang a Broadway show tune, playing and dancing around the table, the whole restaurant paused to watch the spectacle unfolding before them. When the hired musician reached the finale of his song and dropped to one knee before the guest of honor, everyone except the man at the neighboring table broke into spontaneous and gleeful applause. He never looked up from his salad. No matter what happened only inches away from his table, he would not let on that he noticed anything.

I think it must have taken incredible effort on his part to not notice the festive commotion around him. But isn't that the way we sometimes are with God? We blind ourselves to his activity around us while mumbling aloud about how absent he is from our lives.

Earlier this week, my son Damian and I were watching one of my favorite scenes from an old movie, *The Man with Two Brains*. Steve Martin plays the brain surgeon, Dr. Herfarrerer, who has fallen in love with an evil and conniving temptress. Standing before the portrait of his late wife, he asks for guidance. "Just show me a sign. Should I marry her or not? Please show me just a little sign."

Suddenly a cold wind begins to blow, sending an icy chill throughout the room, and a voice wails "Noo, nooo, don't do it. . . ." The wall splits in two, and a portrait spins eerily on the wall faster and faster, saying, "Nooo," while the furnishings crash around the room. Suddenly everything is still and Steve Martin slowly picks himself up and says, "Since you won't show me a sign, I guess it's okay to marry her." And he goes on his way.

Jesus' Struggle to Proclaim the Reality of God's Kingdom

The crowds were gathering, and they seemed on the surface to be interested in his message, but he had the sense that they weren't understanding at all, so he changed tactics. Instead of teaching in a straightforward way, he tried a whole new approach to teaching. His disciples noticed the change and were confused. They wondered why Jesus was telling nice little life stories, illustrations, and parables. Jesus, perhaps sensing their confusion, responded by telling another parable. This one was about a man who planted seeds and in time found a variety of responses to his efforts. Some of the seeds began to grow quickly. But thorns and weeds choked them, and the new plants died. Some seeds landed on the hard path and didn't receive protection from the birds, so they were devoured and never had a chance to take root. Some seeds were baked under the glaring sun and dried up before they could mature. Other seeds landed on fertile ground, took root, and grew to produce fruit. Then Jesus ended his story in a peculiar way, "He who has ears to hear, let him hear" (Mark 4:9).

What Jesus' Struggle Means for Us Today

When we practice denial, it makes no difference what is happening around us; we will see only what we choose to see. Jesus struggled in his efforts to proclaim and demonstrate the reality of God's kingdom in the world. In spite of teaching, healing, arguing, and performing miracles, things did not go smoothly for him. He experienced real difficulties and resistance to his ministry.

What does this mean for us today? Jesus' story gives us four insights that can help us set aside our denial.

We must acknowledge God's rule in our lives. The different kinds of soil in the parable represent the people in our world. There are rocky, thorny, hard people who choose to make themselves impervious to the gospel and refuse to acknowledge God's rule in their lives. Our issue is not to identify who these people are but rather to ask, "Lord, am I the fruitful soil?" Are my life, my mind, my relationships, and my plans open and receptive to God's word so it may penetrate and take root in me?

We must not deny the real world in which we live and the resistance to God's rule wherever it seeks to break through. Remember that when we say this, we are talking about ourselves as well as our own well-entrenched defense systems. We are often as guilty of refusing the standards as those people "out there." We have just become a little more adept at playing the games, so our resistance to God is not so apparent on the surface.

In his book *One-Way Relationships,* Alfred Ells points out that "Sometimes it's easier to deny the severity of the problem rather than to look deeply inside and discover the ugly or painful parts. It hurts to face something painful, but it hurts more not to. The truth hurts, but it will set you free. Denial soothes our senses but keeps us in bondage."

We must not waste time on unresponsive people. This lesson is potentially controversial because it goes against the grain of some of us who have made people pleasing an art form. We struggle with discriminating when it comes to investing our time and energy in needy people, projects, and ministries. Yet Jesus discriminated. He seemed to know when he was wasting his time and refused to buy into the attention-getting demands of those who were not willing to respond or be receptive to the call of discipleship.

I'm sorry to say that I learned this lesson the hard way. In the early years of our marriage, my wife and I struggled tremendously and spent a large number of years and dollars in therapy. But for the first seven years we made little progress because I had a problem; I was in denial.

I didn't think I had a problem; I was a nice guy. I reasoned, "Who wouldn't be happy with someone like me?" So I graciously consented to go to a counselor to help my wife, Eileen, with her problems! I knew how to twist everything so that I was always right. Our life together finally deteriorated to the point where I could no longer ignore the pain or deny the truth. And for the first time I became open to the healing. Until I was willing to be responsive, there was very little that could be done to help me or our marriage.

We usually don't change until we hurt badly enough. Sometimes the most difficult thing for us to do is stand by and watch someone we love sink deeply into a miry pit. We wonder if they will ever hit bottom, and our natural tendency is to jump in and ease their pain. On the surface it makes sense, but it may keep them from breaking through and finally accepting responsibility for themselves and admitting that they have needs. When we admit we have needs, we open the door for health. God reaches out to us at the point of our need and says, "Welcome home."

Like the men and women in Scripture, we can respond to God in a variety of ways. When Moses brought word of God's actions and intentions on behalf of his people, the Bible shows two very different responses to God's message of freedom. Pharaoh said, "Who is the Lord, that I should heed his voice and let Israel go? I do not know the Lord and I will not let Israel go" (Exod. 5:2). But when the people of Israel heard the word of God and saw the miracles, there is a different response: "When they heard that the Lord was concerned about them and had seen their misery, they bowed down and worshipped" (Exod. 4:31, NIV).

I have plenty of good excuses to be distracted and confused. I have justifications for my lack of response to the call of Jesus Christ. Perhaps I don't hurt badly enough to change, or perhaps I'm not ready to admit there's a problem. But if we are willing to be the open soil and ready to begin a new adventure of following Christ on a daily basis, Jesus says, "I stand at the door and knock; if anyone hears my voice and opens the door, I will come in to him" (Rev. 3:20).

We can get very tired of trying to hold it together on our own strength. Remember, it is when we feel stressed and pressured, tired of holding back the tears and fighting against fear and anxiety, Jesus says, "Come to me, all you who are weary and heavy-burdened, and I will give you rest" (Matt. 11:28, NIV).

Change is never easy for me. But I'm beginning to realize that when I hurt badly enough to change and finally set aside my long-protected denial, there is hope for a new beginning.

CHAPTER FOURTEEN

Revealing the Standards: Surrender

> Your strength is your problem. You must learn to control it,
> become weaker.
> SAMURAI WARRIOR IN THE NOVEL *MUSASHI*
> BY YOSHIKAWA

*W*HEN Jesus entered Jerusalem on that first Palm Sunday, everyday life was pretty much the same as life in our own world today. Outwardly it might have looked very different, but people were just like us. Some people were doing well, and others were frustrated with their lives. There were celebrations and sickness, births and deaths, hopes and fears. It was a time of rapid change. Old ways and traditional attitudes and values were giving way to new perspectives and new approaches to life in the modern world.

Like any big city, there was a mix of cultures, nationalities, and religions that made for an interesting exchange of ideas and a rise in strange and exotic teachings. Some people felt a restless longing for someone to come into their lives and fix things or make wrong things right, to rescue them from all those things that made them helpless victims. The military had been strong and successful in battle, the government couldn't be trusted, and many religious leaders were self-seeking and corrupt. Jesus rode into this world on that first Palm Sunday.

By most any standard, Palm Sunday marked the pinnacle of Jesus' success. With every miracle, teaching opportunity, and conflict with the religious authorities, his popularity with ordinary people grew. On the day of his triumphant ride into Jerusalem, the crowds gathered, lining the streets to shout his praise and hail him as the Messiah, the fulfillment of their hopes and dreams. He was a success.

But what is success and how do we measure it? How do we know when we have achieved it? Alfred E. Newman, the poster boy for *MAD* magazine, said, "No one knows what success is, but we are all certain we don't have it."

Mark Twain reminds us, "All you need in this life is ignorance and confidence, and then success is sure."

The True Success of Jesus and His Ministry

If the account of Jesus' life was to end on Palm Sunday, Jesus' mission and ministry in the eyes of most people would have been an overwhelming success. He had achieved fame and public acclamation as well as personal power and visibility for his proclamation of the Kingdom of God. He was a success.

But we must look beyond the surface to find Christ's true success. Have you noticed that Kingdom values are not always the same as worldly values? In fact, wherever we find God's rule in our lives, or his "Kingdom," we discover an almost opposite set of values, priorities, and assumptions confronting us. It can be challenging and even a little disturbing to realize that God's ways are most likely not our ways.

For this reason, Jesus' story doesn't end on Palm Sunday. In fact, it stands in stark contrast to the events that follow a few days after the Palm Sunday parade.

Gone are the exuberant crowds, the palm branches, the triumphant parade, the loud singing, and the heady enthusiasm. In their place is a dark night, a few friends, and our Lord's final temptation to turn aside from his death on the cross. I believe that it was here in the garden, not on the parade route, that Jesus redefined success and revealed the standards once and for all.

Let's look more closely at Matthew's account. First, Jesus is straightforward and honest with the disciples. "He said to them, "You will all fall away because of me this night; for it is written, 'I will strike the shepherd, and the sheep of the flock will be scattered'" (Matt. 26:31). But Peter is indignant and quick to set himself apart from the others. "Though they all fall away because of you, I will never fall away" (Matt. 26:33).

You've got to love Peter. He is so impetuous and enthusiastic, so strong and daring. He is quick to distance himself from the weaker disciples. He is bold, blustery, and persuasive. Filled with self-confidence, self-assurance, self-reliance, and self-control (*self, self, self*), he refuses to hear Jesus' warning and declares, "Even if I must die with you, I will not deny you" (Matt. 26:35).

Our biggest threat comes not from weakness but strength. Peter was about to learn the first lesson for Kingdom living: He is in more danger from his unchecked strengths than his weaknesses. There is a marked difference between Peter's behavior and Jesus'. Jesus openly shared his struggles with a few trusted friends and asked for their help, prayer, and support to see him through his trial. Peter, like so many of us, was not about to admit weakness in front of his friends or in the face of ensuing turmoil. Instead he acted on his own strength, tried to push his way through, and ultimately lost.

Prayer is our greatest offense and our greatest defense. There is a large gap between knowing about prayer and doing it. Even though I know better, I will still try a million things first before prayer. Prayer becomes the tool of last resort rather than my initial response. It seems to come more naturally for me to brood, fuss, and finally strategize possible scenarios long before I will get around to praying. Sometimes when I'm most frustrated, I don't want to pray because I have such a stinky attitude. Now I know that prayer doesn't require a proper attitude or even a clear mind. But old barriers are hard for me to overcome despite my best and worst intentions.

Unfortunately the Church has not helped in this regard. Rather than seeing prayer as a normal and personal dialogue with a friend who knows us intimately and believes in us and loves us for who we are, we have made prayer a distant rumbling of religious jargon.

The first time we have to pray out loud can be a frightening experience. When I was in fourth grade Sunday school, we were told to "go around the circle, with each child praying a short sentence prayer." I was determined not to embarrass myself so I planned ahead and prepared what I would pray for my sentence when it was my turn.

As each person took a turn, I determined that I would pray a simple yet elegant prayer that would have all the important elements of thanksgiving, praise, and adoration and would be ecologically and politically correct. I rehearsed it feverishly in my mind: "Thank you, God, for the trees. . . . Thank you, God, for the trees."

In the back of my mind I could hear the prayers moving around the circle, ever closer to me and my moment of spiritual truth. It was almost my turn to pray. I was ready, confident, and able. One more person and it would be my turn. Next to me, my friend Bobby Dodder sat squirming. It was his turn. I wished he would hurry up and pray so I could do mine. Suddenly he blurted out, "Thank you, God, for the trees. Amen." I was sunk. He stole my prayer, I didn't have a backup, and I was humiliated because everyone would know that I didn't know how to pray effectively.

Somehow we forget that God is not concerned with how we pray, the words we use, or if we do it right. He only cares that we do it. It is not important for us that it is our chance to read God our laundry list of desires, needs, and concerns. Rather, it is important to allow him to show us what he would have us be and what he would have us do.

There is power in letting go. When we try to grasp and control, we inevitably lose. But when we let go we are fulfilled. Sometimes we relate better to the old bumper sticker that says, "If you love something, you must let it go . . . and it will return to you. . . . But if it doesn't come back to you, then hunt it down and destroy it."

Paul encouraged the believers in Philippi to "Have this mind in you that was in Christ Jesus, who though he was in the form of God, did not count equality with God a thing to be grasped, but emptied himself, taking the form of a servant, being born in the likeness of men. And being found in human form, he humbled himself and became obedient unto death, even death on a cross. Therefore God has highly exalted Him . . ." (Phil. 2:5–9).

Notice what this says about Christ. Instead of claiming his rights or demanding what he deserved, he did not grasp or cling to his position and power. Rather he set it aside and took on the form of a servant. The image of emptying ourselves is marvelous because it speaks of pouring ourselves out without reluctance or compulsion, but with willingness and freedom to give up what is rightfully ours.

This is very different from my usual attitudes and behavior. I'm more prone to say things like, "I'm burned out," "I feel so drained," "I just don't have any more to give." And the great classic, "I'm running on empty." My family and co-workers are used to hearing these little self-pitying phrases from me because they know how often I choose to self-pity rather than self-empty. When I'm tired, stressed, sad, or lonely, it's easy for me to get brittle. Then I react as if everyone wants a piece of me and there isn't enough to go around.

When I get in this frame of mind, I regard others with suspicion. I start thinking that someone or something out there is taking more than I have to offer or more than I'm willing to give. This results in a sense of emptiness and a feeling of betrayal and abuse. This is very different from the self-emptying that Christ freely did for us . . . and to which he calls us to do as an act of faithful obedience.

Do you hate to feel used or taken advantage of by others? I sure do. I remember a time when I felt particularly bothered in a relationship because I felt that someone was using me and our relationship for his own benefit. It felt rotten. One day over lunch I told a friend quite clearly how justified I was in feeling taken advantage of.

He smiled a little and suggested that next time, before the person has a chance to use me against my will, I step forward and offer myself for his use. "If you initiate it, you won't feel like a victim. After all, it will be your idea."

I did not want to hear it, but later it made sense. Bruce Larson calls this *eucharing* ourselves. The Eucharist, or the bread and cup of the Last Supper, was Jesus' body and blood that was offered and poured out for us. He offered to us freely as an act of love what we could never take from him. In the same way, we offer ourselves to God for his service and pour ourselves out in an act of surrender.

One of the great mysteries of the Kingdom of God is that we usually fall when we strive to elevate, protect, or glorify ourselves. But when we empty ourselves and surrender to God's will in our lives, he lifts us up. In other words, when we surrender to him, he does for us what we can't do for ourselves.

There is victory in surrendering to God's will. The final lesson of Kingdom living is that there is victory in surrender to

God's will. The gospel writer gives us a glimpse of Jesus struggling personally before ultimately surrendering his own will. "Then he said to them, 'My soul is very sorrowful, even to death'; then going a little further, he fell on his face and prayed, 'My Father, if it is possible, let this cup pass from me; nevertheless, not as I will, but as thou wilt'" (Matt. 26: 36).

Three times Jesus prayed this before he went to meet his accusers. Ironically, this is part of the same prayer he had taught his disciples in Matthew 6. It is the same prayer we repeat regularly in worship called the Lord's Prayer. "Thy will be done on Earth as it is in Heaven." Now in his time of greatest despair and personal pain, he prays, "Nevertheless, thy will be done."

In this moment of weakness, sadness, and loneliness, he surrenders to the will of the Father and forever changes the meaning of success. Jesus' success was ultimately determined not on the parade route of Palm Sunday but in the anguish of the garden where he surrendered his will to the Heavenly Father.

One of my heroes is Dave Dravecky. I watched him pitch with the San Diego Padres and followed his pitching throughout his major league career. Every year I look forward to visiting with him on our radio program. He speaks freely of the transitions in his life as he battled cancer, endured painful surgeries, returned to pitch again, then shattered his arm in what may be the most painful moment in sports television.

In his autobiography, *Comeback,* Dave shares some of the lessons he is learning through this painful process. "I've learned to put my life in God's hands. The hardest part of the last two years has been the uncertainty. I had to learn to do what was within my grasp, one day at a time, and leave control of the rest trustingly to God."

Uncertainty haunts each one of us. There are no guarantees that life will be easy and we will live in comfort and security. So I have the same challenge that Dave faces and that you face. That is the challenge to trust God in the face of uncertainty.

PART IV

Grace
to Enable

CHAPTER FIFTEEN

Relating Grace: The Body of Christ

No one said that any of the things which he possessed was
his own, but they had everything in common . . . and a great
grace was upon them all.
ACTS 4:32, 33

*T*HIS is a tough chapter to write. It's difficult for me to
find the right words to communicate the vital relationship Christians have with each other. When I use words like *the Body of
Christ,* people's eyes glaze over and they fall into cosmic boredom.
Yet the very word *church* is terribly loaded with all kinds of positive
and negative meanings based on our individual experiences. I
don't know how to address this important part of life without
touching on our preconceived ideas, so I'll just blunder along.

We've got to find out what it means for us to be part of the
Church that Paul had in mind when he wrote, "You are the body
of Christ and individually members of it" (1 Cor. 12:27). What is
the Body of Christ, and how do we find our place in it? Through
the years there has been disagreement as to whether the Church
is a living organism or a deadly organization.

Robert Boyd Munger, author of *My Heart, Christ's Home,*
says that some people regard the Church as primarily an organization that every once in a while comes to life, while others see it

as a living, growing organism that every once in a while gets organized.

Perhaps this confusion over the nature of the Church exists because we are prone to lose sight of the dynamic, living body of Christ that the Church was intended to be. Instead we have settled for the poor substitute of a religious organization/social club. If we are going to be alive, the hands and feet of Christ in our world, it is important to understand from Scripture what is involved in being the Church in our world today.

Acts 4:32 describes the life of the early Church by focusing on the unity that was present. "Now the company of those who believed were of one heart and soul" (Acts 4:32). There is a unity of purpose when believers in Jesus Christ come together to worship him. It is not the shallow lowest-common-denominator style of religion that we find in many ecumenical gatherings. It is not the "us four and no more" rigidness that is often a part of separatist groups. Rather it is the freeing and enabling unity of people from many experiences and walks of life, drawn together in the common bond of their commitment to Christ.

Our Need for Community

Unfortunately in the midst of this unity and bonding we can find ourselves feeling confused. We are unsure about our involvement in such a powerful interpersonal relationship with other believers. When it comes to being in community with other Christians, many of us find ourselves feeling ambivalent. I'm ambivalent when I don't know and I'm not sure. When I'm emotionally ambivalent, I feel pulled in two directions at once.

It's easy to say that it is very important to me to belong to a group of friends who know each other and in turn are known for who we are. Yet at the same time, I live in ways that undermine and destroy the very bonds of community I am looking for.

This dilemma is discussed by author Terry Hershey in his book *Stay Away, Come Closer*. It seems that we desire and seek intimacy while we repel people at the same time. This mixed message and the confused emotions that accompany it leave us longing for community on the one hand and avoiding it on the other.

This has become an increasingly widespread phenomena that often results in people feeling torn between conflicting desires. We are left like an emotional version of Dr. Doolittle's two-headed beast, the "Pushme Pullyou." We will discover sufficient motivation to move forward only when our desire for intimacy exceeds our fear of it.

Belonging to a community is not new. In fact, it began with the call to Abraham to step out in faith and follow God with the trust that God would bring him to a place of blessing. The promise was that God would use Abraham to create a community, a great nation, a people of blessing. This then becomes the spiritual roots or heritage of the Church that emerges from the account in Acts. Within the Book of Acts we can identify several marvelous marks of the Church, the community of believers.

We need a place to belong. Some of us try to discover a sense of belonging in our neighborhoods. Where we live or even where we are from can give us an identity that helps us feel as if we belong.

Many of us have come to our cities and towns from very different backgrounds. Some people know other customs and traditions that give them a sense of identity and belonging. While speaking at a conference recently, I met a young man who grew up in a small town in Canada. He said that there was a general acceptance of differences in his hometown. No matter how strange a person was, they were accepted within the community merely because they were there. "We all knew that old man Clarke down the road wasn't right, but we figured that was just the way he was, so he stayed a part of our community."

Ralph Keyes, describing life in a small town in Yorkshire, says that the most striking quality of the town and the thing he misses most is the feeling of being known there. He says that it is not a spoken thing. "Nobody would say anything out loud about your behavior. But they knew, you knew they knew, they knew you knew they knew—and in that there was comfort."

Where do you go to belong? Throughout the years comparisons have been made between the Church and a local bar. Psychiatrist Donald Muhich, in an article in the *Wall Street Journal,* writes, "It sounds like a simple statement, but not everybody realizes that people don't go to bars to drink—they can do that at home and for less money. People go to bars as a social function. Bars can be one of the invisible caretakers of a community, a place where people go to solve problems, meet friends, contract business, kick around ideas, deal with one another. A kind of leaderless group therapy. . . ." This kind of social setting, where people have a place to belong in spite of their troubles or personality quirks, was romanticized in the sitcom "Cheers," which for many years was my favorite television show.

We can learn a lot from bars. Perhaps if our churches were more like bars, we would be more effective at being the Body of Christ. I hope we can discover, as the believers in Acts had, that the Church is a place to belong, share life, and experience healing.

We need a place to share. Acts 4:34 clearly states, "There was not a needy person among them. . . ." Each person contributed as they were led, and provision was made so that everyone's needs were met. We all bring a strange mixture of needs and resources.

The Church can be one place where our strengths and weaknesses merge together. We are not always the needy person who takes and depletes those around us. Nor are we always the strong and invincible person who is always on the lookout for someone less fortunate to help. Rather, we bring what we have and who we are, and find that there is more than enough for everyone. In effect, we share because we are all part of the team.

Magic Johnson, longtime star of the Los Angeles Lakers, was credited with an unusual type of assist prior to his retirement when he tested positive for the HIV virus. He voluntarily gave up a significant part of his salary so the Lakers could acquire a new player under the NBA salary cap requirements.

Johnson, who was named MVP for the third time, said he was willing to give up a substantial portion of his salary to strengthen his team. "It's about winning. Of course, money is great," he said, "but I play to win and that's why I did it."

We need a place to encourage. In the Acts, Luke singled out one person who seemed to be a living symbol of what was happening in the Church as a whole. Joseph was nicknamed "Barnabus" by the other disciples. Luke tells us that the name meant "Son of Encouragement." He writes, "Thus Joseph who was surnamed Barnabus, sold a field which belonged to him, and brought the money and laid it at the apostles' feet" (Acts 4:36).

This is the first of many references to Barnabus in the Book of Acts. He seemed to be a walking example of Christian living as he gave freely, invested himself in others, and nurtured and encouraged people. He repeatedly put his trust in people on whom others had given up and found a way to affirm the good and enable others to be stronger than they thought they were.

"The world around us is filled with discouraged people who desperately need encouragement," Lloyd Ogilvie reminds us in his book *Drumbeat of Love*. "Body life is the fellowship of the sons (and daughters) of encouragement. There is no new name we need more than this one given to Joseph. (As a church) we are to stand with each other, liberating each other with Christ's love and energizing each other with his immense availability."

We need a place to tell the truth. Luke always dealt with reality. He lets us know that everything was not completely wonderful in the early Church. And it is not always wonderful today. We are still people of mixed motives and sinful hearts. The account of Annanias and Saphira (Acts 5) reminds us that pretense and dishonesty undermine the very relationships we want to nurture.

They were under no compulsion to give this apparently generous gift to the Church. But in order to look good and gain power and favor in the community, they plotted a scheme to defraud the family. The shock and guilt of being exposed as grifters apparently led to their sudden and unexpected deaths.

It also sent shock waves through the Church. People heard the clear message that it is a place where people are honest with themselves, with God, and with each other. It's not always easy or comfortable to be in community like this. But it is the only way to live because when we are honest, we become free.

Several top executives in Seattle are learning that they need this kind of honest exchange. They have joined a membership organization for chief executive officers called The Executive Committee. They attend an all-day meeting once a month and pay $1,800 per quarter to participate.

There are many benefits cited for participants in the group, but what they like most is the chance to be told the brutal, ugly truth once in a while. "There are not a lot of people willing to tell that to the president of the company," one member says.

They are the elite of the business community, and they don't have to answer to anyone. However, deep down, they all crave accountability. "People look up to you for all this worldly advice," says one member. "Sometimes the CEO needs advice, too."

It isn't the issue whether or not we are the business elite. All of us need honest feedback and accountability. Not only will the Church benefit from being more like a bar; we could also take a lesson from accountability groups like The Executive Committee.

In his book *Travels with Charlie,* John Steinbeck calls beauty parlor employees the most influential people in the community. "When women go to the hairdresser, something happens to them. They feel safe, they relax. And they don't have to keep up any pretense. The hairdresser knows what their skin is like under the makeup, he knows their age, their face-liftings. This being so, women tell a hairdresser things they wouldn't dare confess to a priest, and they are more open about matters they'd try to conceal from a doctor." Perhaps this is why the hair care ad on TV said, "Only my hairdresser knows for sure."

We need a place to grow. When the Church is healthy, functioning as the body of Christ, people who want something easy, undemanding, and cheap will turn away feeling uncomfortable about the expectations and accountability that is involved in being the Church. At the same time, however, the Church will find itself growing both in terms of numbers of people and in the quality of life in the Body.

Growth is the natural by-product of faithfully following Jesus Christ. People are often surprised at the effort that people must make to become members of our Church. There are many hurdles to get over because we want involvement to be as meaningful as it can possibly be. You and I don't stop growing when we join the Church either. Who I am continues to be shaped and refined as I grapple with real life and apply my faith in tangible ways to the issues around me.

We need a place to heal. My mental image of a church usually has many well-dressed, healthy, successful-looking people gathering around to impress each other with their outward appearance.

Of course, this is not a biblical picture of the Church. As the Church grows it never remains solely the haven of the healthy. In fact, the stronger it becomes, the more it attracts those who are in need of healing. The Church will always resemble a hospital more than a country club. We will inevitably find ourselves facing great opportunities for healing.

Because of this, ministry is never going to be neat, tidy, or predictable. Rather it is often messy, disturbing, and out of control. In fact, the only way we will ever become the Church that we are meant to be is through a miracle from God himself. But that is the point, isn't it?

CHAPTER SIXTEEN

Rescuing Grace: Salvation

God so loved the world that he sent his only son that
whoever believes in him should not perish but have
eternal life.

JOHN 3:16

SALVATION is a loaded word. It brings to mind all kinds
of feelings, thoughts, and experiences from the past. When we
see the word *saved,* it immediately conjures up a variety of positive and negative images. When good and bad experiences fight
their way to the surface of our minds, we may be prevented from
clearly hearing what God has to say to us.

For some people, being saved is the best news they could
imagine. Perhaps they feel trapped, discouraged, confused, helpless, or desperate. They can relate to the writer of Psalm 40 who
felt as if he were sinking in an overwhelming pit of oozing muck.
He said, "The Lord heard my cry and lifted me out of the miry
bog, out of the pit and put my feet on a solid rock, made my
steps secure and put a new song in my mouth" (paraphrase). It is
a welcome relief to know that there is a God who hears our cry
when we are in over our heads and who acts out of love to get us
back on our feet. This is good news.

Some of us, however, have images of salvation that don't seem like good news. I know people who feel coerced, demeaned, insulted, and judged when told about following Christ. When they hear about salvation, it is in the tone of fear and judgement rather than the context of God's overwhelming love and grace. This leaves them regretful or resentful of the circumstances that led to their commitment.

When my wife was five years old, she was taken to a "tent meeting" revival. There she was shown graphic pictures of Satan and his demons. "If you don't let Jesus into your heart," she was warned, "the devil will devour you for all eternity!"

Later that evening, while riding home in the car, she was overwhelmed with terror and broke down in tears. "Mommy, I don't want to be eaten by the devil. What can I do to be saved?" So, there in the car on that dark, scary night she prayed that Jesus would come into her life and keep her from the evil clutches of Satan.

"All of my life," Eileen says, "I have regretted the way in which I became a Christian. It was not until I was thirty-two years old that I realized God loved me. My relationship with God was essentially fear-oriented." It is sad that many sincere followers of Christ begin their Christian experience rooted in fear, guilt, and anxiety, not grounded in the overwhelming love of God.

Some of us struggle on a different side of the salvation issue. We have a terrible time admitting that we are lost. We don't like to show weakness or face the reality that we are unable to overcome every obstacle in our path.

Ever since I was a little child, my parents warned me of the dangers of getting lost. Though I wasn't sure what it meant to be lost, I was absolutely convinced that whatever it was, I would not let it happen to me. When I was four years old, my family visited friends in a nearby city. I had a spur-of-the-moment urge to explore the neighborhood. Without telling anyone, I quietly toddled out of the house and began my daring adventure, confident that I would never be so foolish as to get lost.

After crossing several streets, turning corners, and exploring the adventure possibilities of this strange neighborhood, it suddenly dawned on me that I didn't know where I was, where the house was, or which direction I should go to find my way back. The houses began to look very much alike, and I was sure that I had been gone an immeasurable amount of time and had travelled a vast distance.

As tears began to roll down my pudgy cheeks, I did the bravest thing I could think of—I walked faster. That way I could at least fool people into thinking that I knew where I was going. Passing a house, I noticed two older children playing in the driveway. A girl who looked about twelve noticed my tears and called out, "Little boy, are you lost?"

"No," I cried, "I'm not lost!" Then I began to run down the sidewalk as fast as my little legs could carry me.

The girl wouldn't give up. "Mom, come quick. There is a little boy out here and he is lost."

"I'm not lost!" I screamed over my shoulder.

Immediately the concerned mother telephoned her neighbors farther down the block to be on the lookout for a little lost boy so they could intercept me. With half a dozen neighbors in pursuit calling out to me, "Come back, we want to help!" and me screaming, "I'm not lost!" I suddenly rounded the corner and miraculously saw my brothers playing in the yard of the home we were visiting. Imagine my parents' surprise when I raced through the front door yelling, "I'm not lost!"

Think of what happens to us as adults when we have the mindset that refuses to acknowledge that we are lost. We hear God say, "I've come to find you in your lostness, in your hurt, in your confusion. I've come to show you the way home." Yet we stubbornly insist, "I am not lost. I can find my own way. I can make it on my own."

Unfortunately, our attitudes, experiences, and preconceived ideas block what God wants to do. We refuse to allow him to show us the truth about ourselves, himself, and salvation. We cannot allow our past experiences and present attitudes or prejudices to blind us to the truth about God and ourselves.

What is the truth? According to the Bible, there are several things that are true. One of these truths is that God is in the business of giving us life—full, abundant, exciting, meaningful, eternal life. Jesus said, "I came that they may have life, and have it abundantly" (John 10:10). He also said, "I am the resurrection and the life" (John 11:25). In John 14:6, he said, "I am the way, and the truth and the life; no one comes to the Father but by me." Paul wrote in Ephesians 2:1, "And you he made alive." What does it mean to be saved? It means that we become one of the alive ones. Christians are those whom God has made alive.

Paul then describes the problem in which we find ourselves. The problem is, "You were dead through the trespasses and sins in which you once walked, following the course of this world" (Eph. 2:1, 2).

Sometimes we don't want to admit there is a problem. We want to be left alone in our misery and self-deception. We may be going through the motions of life. We may continue to act according to our desires and drives. We may show up for meetings and appointments. But we are not really living.

The good news is linked with what may be the most powerful two words ever written, *But God*. Whatever else has happened, no matter how lost we are, no matter what mess we have made of our lives, no matter what outward signs of success we have achieved to cover the hollow emptiness inside, God has the intervening last word.

Paul writes, "But God, who is rich in mercy, out of the great love with which he loved us, even when we were dead through our trespasses, made us alive together with Christ (by grace you have been saved)" (Eph. 2:4).

Notice what this tells us about God. He is rich in mercy. He has a great love toward us. He loves us as much when we are dead in our sins as when we are alive in him. And his love is unconditional.

Contrary to what many of us were led to believe, God is not a stern, angry judge who looks down at us with scorn and disapproval. He is not a cosmic policeman who flashes spiritual red lights in our rearview mirrors. Neither is he the punishing parent figure that we were warned about when we were told, "Wait until your father gets home. Then you'll really get what's coming to you." These are all unbiblical ideas about God that have somehow seeped into our minds and colored our perspectives.

We need a fresh look at the God in Scripture who is full of mercy and relentless in his love for each of us. We will always keep our guard up and be stiff, formal, standoffish, and fundamentally frightened in our relationship with God until we discover his love.

We need a key to unlock our relationship with Jesus Christ. I believe the key is in the word *grace*. Throughout this book we see that grace (God's free gift, unmerited favor, unearned blessing) is at the heart of God's involvement in our lives.

As we look at our own need for salvation and God's loving action to rescue us and give us new life, we are once more face-to-face with grace.

Grace is the source of our salvation. It is a free gift from God. It can't be bought or bartered, nor can it be exchanged or sold. It can only be accepted or refused. Grace is our undeserved and unmerited standing with God. It is not a reward for a lifetime of faithfulness and service, nor is it a merit badge that indicates we have arrived at a particular status or level of achievement.

Nicodemus, a leader of people, came secretly to Jesus at night to ask what it took to be part of God's kingdom. Jesus reminded him of a time in the history of the Hebrew people when they wandered in the wilderness and poisonous snakes took over the camp and threatened the lives of all the people. In Numbers 21, God tells Moses to make a bronze serpent and hold it up on a banner pole. Anyone who had been bitten by the snakes would be healed and would live if they would simply look up at the bronze serpent. Jesus then tells Nicodemus, "In the same way I will be lifted up, so that whoever believes in me will have eternal life" (John 3:14, 15, paraphrase).

We'll never know how Nicodemus responds to Jesus' words. But it doesn't take much imagination to realize that we are not very different from the Hebrew people in the wilderness. We tend to be sick, tired, and dying. We live with a certain amount of pain and joy mixed together.

Picture Moses lifting high the bronze serpent, calling to the people, "Look up and live! If you only have enough faith to lift your eyes from your problems and trust God's promise, you will be healed."

I'm sure some of the people scowled and murmured, "What crazy idea does Moses have now? I'm not going to look up at a stupid statue. Besides, some of us are fed up with him asking us to do unreasonable things just because he thinks God is talking to him. If Moses says we need to do this, well, that's reason enough to turn away."

Others were too religious to look up. Perhaps they were sophisticated, theological people who debated the relative appropriateness of Moses' making a statue in the first place. A statue of a serpent is even worse. "Besides," they probably muttered, "this is simply not the way it's done in our tradition. We won't look up because we have never done it this way before."

Then there were those who were preoccupied with their condition, their pressing needs, and the very real pain. They were lost in the immediate hurt that seemed so overpowering. "I can't look up; I'm in too much pain," they probably cried. "Can't you see how sick I am? How could Moses be so insensitive that he would ask one more thing of me?"

But a few listened to God's promise and in faith looked up at the serpent and felt the poison drain from their pain-ridden bodies. They felt the strength return to their limbs, and they felt new life as God in his grace healed them according to his word.

"In the same way," Jesus says, "whoever believes in me may have eternal life" (John 3:15).

In the movie *Indiana Jones: The Last Crusade,* Indiana stands on the edge of a cliff high above a ravine. He must get across, but there is absolutely no way to cross to the other side. Suddenly he does what seems completely crazy. He swallows hard and steps out into midair. As he puts his foot down, a path suddenly appears supporting him step-by-step across the ravine. Like Indiana Jones, we too must step out into the uncertain and the unknown. That is what faith is all about.

Faith is our willingness to let go of the controls of our lives and trust God minute-by-minute. It is our willingness to step out, knowing that we don't have enough information, preparation, or perspiration to get by, and trust him anyway. And he is there.

CHAPTER SEVENTEEN

Releasing Grace: Spiritual Gifts

Now about spiritual gifts, I do not want you to be ignorant.
1 CORINTHIANS 12:1, NIV

"**I** am in way over my head," I confided to a friend. "It's apparent to me, and I suspect it will be obvious to others very soon." I shared how I became involved in a challenging project that at first I was confident I could handle. Now reality was setting in and I knew I didn't have what it takes to succeed, much less survive. After listening, my friend leaned back in his chair and said, "If this depends on you and your abilities, you're toast. I think it will take a miracle to pull this off." Then he leaned forward and with a laugh asked, "Have you ever seen what God can do when you finally run out of ideas?"

I began to wonder if perhaps one of the reasons I see very little spiritual power in my life is that I don't allow myself to climb far enough out on the ledge to really need him and the spiritual gifts he offers.

Perhaps no other aspect of the Christian life has been so studied, discussed, and debated. It has potential to disrupt and tear apart the unity of the church, while at the same time it has great potential to unite and release the people in creative and loving ministry. In spite of hundreds of books being written on the subject, seminars and conferences held, and sermons preached about spiritual gifts, there is still widespread ignorance and misunderstanding.

Before I go on, let me warn that I do not address the relative merits of specific gifts in this chapter. Rather I write about being spiritually gifted. The biblical idea of giftedness is a broad and diverse illustration of God's equipping his people for service. While Paul refers to gifts of healing, teaching, and leadership, the Old Testament refers to spiritual gifts of jewelry making and wood carving. The common thread is that we all are gifted by God to live beyond our natural abilities.

What Are Spiritual Gifts?

The Greek word that most often refers to spiritual gifts in the New Testament is *charisma*. That word has leaked its way into our vocabulary in ways that go beyond the biblical meaning. For example, we say, "She is so strong, confident, and attractive; she obviously has charisma." When charisma was used to describe John F. Kennedy, it was the first time that word had been applied to a president of the United States. *Charisma* is a word that in our contemporary culture has lost much of its spiritual bearing and has come to symbolize an attitude of confidence and surety. It has come to signify less of a spiritual reality and more of a force of personality.

For Christians there is a more significant meaning to the word. The root of the word is *charis* and means "grace." Thus charisma is the tangible provision of grace or the gift from God of spiritual power to enable us to accomplish what he calls us to do. Spiritual gifts are God's way of releasing us to accomplish his will.

It is very easy for me to feel frustrated, stressed, or even burned out as I go along. Sometimes I even get the mistaken idea that God's will must be the hard, difficult, or distasteful thing. Old tapes play in my mind telling me that I had better be careful or I will be exposed as being inadequate for the task.

I have become a bit of an expert at covering up and hiding my insecurity and pretending I'm in control. But inside I feel my stomach tightening and the pressure building because I know the truth: On my own, I don't have the strength, wisdom, or energy to accomplish what I am called to do.

God understands that we don't have the ability to live the Christian life apart from a relationship with Jesus Christ. It was never intended to be that way. Furthermore, it is never God's will that we burn out in ministry. You can do it if you want, but it is not what God intended when he called us to follow him. Some churches, and even some pastors, have worn their stress like a trophy. Their message appears to be, "Please feel sorry for us, look at how hard we work." It is almost as if they think God won't be able to get anything done without them.

One of the churches in which I grew up used to have a special song. The pastors would sing as a quartet with the choir behind them:

> Let me burn out for thee, dear Lord,
> Let me burn out for thee.
> Don't let me rust or my life be a failure,
> Just let me burn out for thee.

Why Are Spiritual Gifts Important?

God doesn't want us to be a bunch of burned-out, tired, defeated, discouraged, and overstressed people. He came to give us life abundant, marked by joy and fulfillment. Being burned out is a sign that there is something wrong. Workaholism is a sin. Allowing our ministries to grind us up is missing the mark. Trying to do it all is unbiblical.

All of this happens because we are either ignorant or not utilizing the gifts—the charisma the Holy Spirit offers to us as Christians. We must rediscover God's strategy and resources for releasing us in ministry.

Spiritual gifts are given to every Christian. Paul writes, ". . . it is the same God who inspires them all in every one. To each is given the manifestation of the Spirit . . ." (1 Cor. 12:6, 7). Spiritual gifts are never the marks of the elite, the super saints, or the inner circle. Every believer has been gifted to minister in Jesus' name. When we hold back saying, "I'm not gifted," we call God a liar and turn away from the gift he offers to us.

Spiritual gifts are for the common good. Gifts are given not as trophies to gather dust on our mantles or to provide an interesting topic to banter about in the halls. Paul writes, "To each is given a manifestation of the Spirit for the common good" (1 Cor. 12:7). The benefit of having spiritual gifts is twofold. It benefits us personally because we are empowered to serve beyond our natural abilities or limitations. But it also benefits others as the gifts are used to encourage, enable, and empower them.

There are no second-class Christians. Paul is quick to point out in Scripture that everyone has a place in the Body of Christ. We don't rank each other and say that one is more important than the other. "If the whole body were an eye, where would be the hearing? And if the whole body were an ear, where would be the sense of smell?" (1 Cor. 12:17). In the Body of Christ there is room for everyone, and everyone has a place. Being part of the body means that if we are healthy, we function without regard for which job or person is more or less significant.

We are gifted for a purpose. That purpose is the building up of others in the Body of Christ. Christians have traditionally struggled with the tension between *being* and *doing*. Some would say that what matters is that we just *be* in our relationship with Christ. One of my friends who is a pastor of a large church believes that the church is like a giant cruise ship. "When you're out in the ocean," he says, "it doesn't matter which direction you are sailing. What counts is that everyone is having a good time aboard the ship."

I pointed out to him that when we align ourselves too far toward the *being* side of the continuum, we can become purposeless. We end up reducing ministry to the maintenance of a "happy camper" style of Christianity.

The other side of the continuum is the *doing* side. Years ago this produced the Protestant work ethic in which accomplishments became the measure of faithfulness. People thought that through our busyness we would glorify God. We were warned that "Idleness is the devil's playground." Our faith turned into the justification for workaholism and other obsessive behaviors.

Neither of these extremes is God's intention. We are not adrift, nor are we busy little spiritual bees who do good things for God. Rather, we are secure in relationship with the Lord so we rest in him (being), and we are called to follow him in purposeful life-changing ministry (doing).

Spiritual gifts are meant to be used. It is possible to spend so much time studying and analyzing spiritual gifts that we never use them for the purposes they were given. Perhaps this is why Paul wrote, "If a person's gift is prophesying, let him use it in proportion to his faith. If it is serving, let him serve; if it is teaching, let him teach; if it is encouraging, let him encourage; if it is contributing to the needs of others, let him give generously; if it is leadership, let him govern diligently; if it is showing mercy, let him do it cheerfully" (Rom. 12:6–8, NIV). In other words, whatever your gift—just do it!

We all face the very real danger of losing our spiritual balance. In ministry we can become unbalanced when either of two things happens.

The first danger is giving on our own resources without allowing God to fill and refill us with his grace and power. I sure know how it feels to get out of balance in this way. First, I begin to feel alone, as if I am the only one making an effort. In my mind everyone else seems too selfish to care. Then I get tired and begin to feel a bit self-righteous. After all, what a sacrifice I am making! Then the bitterness and envy start to set in, and I start spiraling into a deep spiritual funk. It's not pretty, but from time to time, we all find ourselves in this predicament.

I was in one of these moods a while ago. I had overextended myself and begun to lose perspective of who was in control. Assuming I was perfectly fine, I went away to a cabin in the mountains where I had planned to have a little spiritual getaway. Wanting to act religious and mature, I had planned to try praying, studying, and doing other so-called disciplines. My family left me alone during the day so I could have quality time alone for reflection and prayer.

When they returned that evening, they were probably expecting to find St. John, but I was in a deep depression. I felt sorry for myself and proceeded to moan and groan about how I will never be able to preach another sermon again, I'm too depressed, God can't use me, etc. My wife, Eileen, in her sensitive, loving way, took one look at me and said, "Cut it out! Quit feeling sorry for yourself. Besides, you aren't supposed to be able to preach on your own strength anyway. God is involved in this too, you know." (I hate it when she's right.)

If we could do ministry on our own, we would never need him. Then we would never know that he is there for us and that his grace is sufficient for us. We need his continual refilling in order to take the next step to which he calls us.

The second danger is our refusal to act according to the gift he has given us. We in the church are set free when in faith we all act according to our gifts and participate in the building up of the body. Unfortunately, we can become spiritually constipated by not using our gifts in ministry.

It's possible for me to come to church, study the Bible, worship, and learn all about being a Christian. I can sit for years taking it all in. I can be challenged, encouraged, and nourished, but never give out anything.

We can become like the Dead Sea, where water flows in but none goes out. The result is that we find ourselves rotting in our own spiritual satisfaction.

Spiritual health is dependent on the constant flow of the spirit. We receive and are built up; we serve and build up others. Like breathing out and breathing in, there is a give-and-take to the exercise of our spiritual gifts.

Who we are is more important than what we do. Paul ends both his discussions of spiritual gifts by focusing on love. "But love must be sincere" (Rom. 12:9, NIV). "I will show you a still more excellent way" (1 Cor. 12:31). Then he begins the well-known discourse on love.

Spiritual gifts are not an end in themselves but builders of character. Our character becomes a reflection of the love within us that we extend to one another.

When all is said and done regarding spiritual gifts, what matters is that I be a person of character. Then God can mold me into his image. When confident of his overwhelming love and acceptance toward us, we find ourselves free to be givers of grace out of hearts filled with love. We become men and women who possess true charisma.

CHAPTER EIGHTEEN

Restoring Grace: Forgiveness

Forgiving is love's toughest work, and love's biggest risk.
LEWIS SMEDES

If we confess our sins, he is faithful and just, and will forgive
our sins and cleanse us from all unrighteousness.
1 JOHN 1:9

*H*AD a fight and hurt the one you love? . . . Need to apologize? Just call Apology Accepted. Recently, a young entrepreneur in California turned our need for forgiveness into a business opportunity by founding a company called Apology Accepted. For a fee, his company will apologize and ask forgiveness for you. Owner Loren Harris says, "We're the Pierre Cardin of apology. Whatever it takes, we provide—from a box of chocolates to a yacht."

Forgiveness is a universal need. According to the Bible, our need for forgiveness may be the one element that unites all of humankind. Paul writes to the Christians in Rome, "All have sinned and fall short of the glory of God" (Rom. 3:23). John tells us, "If we say we have no sin, we deceive ourselves, and the truth is not in us" (1 John 1:8). Most of us seem to recognize this in an abstract way. It is certainly something we believe in a theological

sense. It may even be a truth that we can acknowledge on a soci-
ological level. But the crying, desperate need to forgive and to
accept forgiveness is most often buried deep beneath our hard-
ened layers of hurt, insecurity, and fear. In order to live free—un-
encumbered by failures and disappointments—we must first
unlock the secret to forgiveness.

Sometimes we don't want to forgive; we would rather get
even or get back at the person who wronged us. In New York, a
weekly shopper called the *Manhattan Pennysaver* has developed a
new form of advertising called *antipersonals*. Readers are invited to
"give the gift of hate" by placing ads that cut offenders down to
size. In typical New York fashion, the paper urges readers to "Slay
a rotten neighbor. Bad-mouth the public figure of your choice.
Spew forth your anger. You'll feel much better afterwards."

In spite of our best efforts to avoid or achieve forgiveness, it
remains our best resource for the healing and health of our
strained personal relationships and our everyday encounters.
"Forgiving is love's toughest work, and love's biggest risk,"
writes Lewis Smedes. "If you twist it into something it was never
meant to be, it can make you a doormat or an insufferable ma-
nipulator."

It is hard to forgive because we have all been let down and
injured deep in the recesses of our hearts. Sometimes it is easier
for me to cover the hurt and try to move on than to admit the
pain and do the work of forgiveness.

Each of us could write a book about the injustices we have
committed or that have been done to us and those we love. This
story is repeated in our families and relationships over and over
again. Someone cheats me out of what I have coming. I suffer in
ways that I don't deserve. I hurt those I love and inflict pain on
people around me who don't deserve it. Sometimes the pain is
inflicted intentionally and sometimes accidently. But pain is still
pain, and wounds go deep.

When someone hurts us accidently or out of stupidity, it calls to mind the words of Jesus as he was dying on the cross, "Father, forgive them, for they know not what they do" (Luke 23:34). But what about the hurt that results from meanness, conniving, or intentional abuse? How can we discover the courage to forgive these offenses?

We Can Learn to Forgive

Our ability to forgive or accept forgiveness may be the key to living in authentic freedom and grace. We struggle with forgiveness because we have a built-in tension between getting what we deserve and allowing grace to permeate our lives.

Each of us has an internal gauge that monitors the fairness of life. We take in information and run it through our "fairness grid" to see if the behavior, reaction, comment, or treatment is deserved.

Sometimes this is evaluated very intentionally, as when Dietrich Bonhoeffer struggled over the ethical implications of murdering Adolph Hitler. He decided as a Christian that it is wrong to kill a man, but that in this instance it would be a greater wrong to let the man continue to live. So he joined a plot to assassinate Adolph Hitler.

Some events in life are evaluated with a more guttural response. A man drives home from work one winter night in Seattle and a young teenager drops a football-size boulder off a bridge, smashing the windshield, killing the man, and leaving a stunned wife and family. Most people would agree that he didn't deserve it. Or a teenage girl who is tired of being teased by a classmate goes to his house, rings the doorbell, and when he answers, pulls out a gun and shoots him, leaving a shocked family and community wondering how this could have happened. He didn't deserve it.

Our sense of justice also comes into play when we assume that people sometimes do get what they deserve. Authorities in Canton, Georgia, reported that a man was gored to death by his goat. The Cherokee County coroner reported that Carl Hulsey had owned the goat for the past year and beat it regularly with sticks to make it aggressive with people. He was prodding the goat with a stick when the goat chased him and butted him to death.

Perhaps one of the great obstacles to experiencing the richness of forgiveness is that we have a distorted belief about what we deserve. Deep inside, most people carry the gnawing awareness that we really deserve more. No matter how good life is, we are entitled to a bit more, a bit better than we have.

In the movie *City Slickers,* Billy Crystal plays a character who is depressed on his thirty-ninth birthday. His wife tries to console him by showing him what a good life they have, but Billy will hear none of it. He says, "I have a feeling that this is as good as I'm going to feel, as good as I'm going to look, and as good as my life is going to get. But frankly, it's just not that good."

No matter how good or bad our lives have become, they probably won't be good enough. There will always be regrets, offenses, and failures to remind us that we are just not that good. We deserve better. But we also suspect that better probably won't be good enough.

We need a healthy dose of grace. In grace, God gives us what we don't deserve. In grace, we get what we don't have coming. In grace, we discover the fulfillment of our restless longings. And in grace, we find the courage to forgive and to be forgiven.

What will it take for us to know forgiveness in our lives? It begins when we realize that we are the ones who need to be forgiven.

We are needy. Genesis 32 shows us an example of a person coming to terms with his own need for forgiveness. Jacob was terrified when he heard that he was about to come face-to-face with his brother Esau, whom he had cheated, abused, robbed, and shamed. Over twenty years had passed since they had seen each other, but Jacob's guilt for the wrong he had done hung in the air like a putrid mist. Jacob had to face his own well-deserved guilt before he could experience the restoring power of forgiveness.

Jacob prayed, "I am not worthy of the least of all the steadfast love and all the faithfulness which thou hast shown to thy servant" (Gen. 32:10). As long as we continue to defend our rightness, we will never know forgiveness. When we acknowledge our weakness, we are freed to experience and extend grace.

This is why confession has played such an important role in the life of Christians throughout history. What at first glance may appear to be an undo infusion of negativity is in fact the very thing that opens us to receive the gracious gift of forgiveness.

"To confess your sins to God is not to tell him anything he doesn't already know," Frederick Buechner, in his book *Wishful Thinking,* reminds us. "Until you confess them, however, they are the abyss between you. When you confess them, they become the bridge."

Jacob could have prayed very differently. He could have defended himself, shifted the blame, or made excuses. His prayer could have been more like this: "Lord, we all know that I cheated my brother, but consider the circumstances. He didn't care about the inheritance, or he wouldn't have traded it for the quick meal. Besides, it wasn't completely my fault. After all, it was my mother who had the idea in the first place. She really is the one to blame. And Lord, remember how tough it's been these past twenty years. I have had to endure more than my share of abuse at the hands of a conniving and evil father-in-law. I paid my dues; now I have a right to be treated better. I shouldn't have to hide from my brother; he should show me a little respect. Besides, I went out and made something of my life. Who does he think he is, anyway? You know I have rights, too. I deserve better than this."

Until we come to grips with our own need, forgiveness will allude us.

God promises good. Perhaps one of the reasons that forgiveness is so difficult is that we don't believe that God will bring good to us. Therefore we try to keep score, clinging to hurts, fears, and failures. Some of us don't believe God's promises of good because our own guilt and remorse piles up until it blocks our view. We think the blessings of God are for others but not for us. Surely there are those more worthy, more deserving, and more capable than we. God will bless them, not us.

Jacob reminded God of the good that had been promised. "But thou didst say, I will do you good . . . " (Gen. 32:12). We, too, can claim the promises of God in Scripture and trust him to faithfully love us and bless us as his children. One of the verses of the hymn "Amazing Grace" meant a lot to Eileen and me when we were going though a particularly difficult time in our lives. It says:

> The Lord has promised good to me.
> His word my hope secures.
> He will my shield and portion be,
> as long as life endures.

When we feel that this is as good as it gets and that it isn't good enough, we have a tendency to hold back. But when we know that God has promised good to us and it will be good enough, we can be flagrant in forgiveness because we will not lose power, joy, or peace. When we forgive, we only lose pain, sorrow, and rage.

Forgiveness is a gift. Jacob, like any of us who have made our way in the world by use of our negotiating power, thought up a great strategy. He sent drove after drove of gifts ahead of him, with instructions for the people to tell Esau that they were presents from Jacob, who would be arriving soon. The theory was that he could wear down his brother's anger and gain an edge in the certain conflict that was to come.

But Jacob missed the whole point. When the two brothers finally met, "Esau ran to meet him, and embraced him, and fell on his neck and kissed him, and they wept" (Gen. 33:4). Then Esau asks what was the meaning of all the company he met on the road. Jacob tells him it was so he might find favor. Then Esau says, "I have enough, my brother; keep what you have for yourself" (Gen. 33:9).

Jacob didn't understand that forgiveness could neither be extracted nor bartered. Forgiveness is something we give freely for the sake of our own health and sometimes for the health of a relationship. Too often we end up the loser because we've chosen to withhold forgiveness. We might, for example, want someone to suffer sufficiently before we forgive them for the wrong they did us. Unfortunately, they never seem to suffer quite enough. Sometimes they don't even realize they are supposed to be suffering. Yet we stay fixed firmly in the pain of the past, unable or unwilling to heal and move on.

Without cutting any deals, you can give a special gift to someone. You can make the choice to forgive someone for a wrong that was committed, a hurt that you endured, or a mistake that was made. Perhaps the person you choose to forgive will never know that forgiveness has taken place. Like Jacob, he or she may dread seeing you because you know the truth.

Maybe the person you need to forgive is you. You also know the truth about yourself, the hurts you have caused, intentionally or accidently, the stupidities that have haunted you, and the regrets for things you have done or not done. If you think you have suffered enough, maybe it's time to cut the burden loose and forgive yourself.

We have enough. When we withhold forgiveness, it usually is because we want something more. "Something more" could be better treatment, greater rewards, revenge, security, or emotional payoffs. If we are dissatisfied, it is difficult to be gracious.

Esau's answer to his brother Jacob was "I have enough, my brother; keep what you have for yourself" (Gen. 33:9). And Jacob responded, "Accept my gift that is brought to you, because God has dealt graciously with me, and because I have enough" (Gen. 33:11). What a powerful exchange this is. Two brothers whose relationship was severed by greed and deceit now restored by grace. Each is set free when he realizes he has enough.

It is important to see that when we accept ourselves as the unique people God created, loves, and blesses, the door to healing swings open. If we have enough, our losses can be forgiven. If we have enough love, personal slights can be forgiven. If we have enough resources to meet our needs, it becomes possible to forgive those who would cheat us or steal from us. If we have enough, we can more easily forgive those who wound or betray us. If we have enough, we find forgiveness to restore and heal all the broken parts of our life.

Epilogue:
Grace to Satisfy

WHEN I was growing up, there were two things that helped shape me into the person I am today. *Why Johnny Can't Read* was my early reading textbook, which I thought had been published just for me. For years I wondered how they knew I couldn't read. Did my mom call the publisher and let them know? The second influence was "I Can't Get No . . . Satisfaction" by the Rolling Stones. That song hit me right in my young teenage heart and expressed the restless yearning that was spinning deep inside me.

Perhaps I should have combined these influences and titled this book *Why Johnny Can't Get No . . . Satisfaction!* After all, so much of my life has been the search of my own restless heart. Sometimes my efforts to find satisfaction led me into exciting and joyful experiences, and other times it led to lonely, empty places. In every situation I realize now that God was there with me.

"Will you let me be your satisfaction?" he asks me. The fulfillment of my restless search lies in my answer to that question. How can I answer unless I know what I want? I'm like the man in the old Nabisco cracker ad who was rummaging through his refrigerator late at night. "What are you hungry for," asks the announcer, "when you don't know what you're hungry for?"

I have longings and hungers that I can't even identify, but they lead me to browse through the refrigerator of life just to see if there is something there I might have overlooked. It may be a surprise under the tinfoil or a forgotten treat in the back of the freezer. Who knows what may be there for me? Like you, I'm probably a typical, average, searching person who just wants to be happy.

How We See Ourselves

George Barna, one of our nation's foremost marketing research specialists, says that the average American adult perceives herself or himself to be an intelligent, busy, and capable individual. In general, we think of ourselves as religious but not overbearing in our beliefs. We see ourselves as conservative more than liberal. We would say we are decent, moral persons—more ethically sound than we ever dreamed we would become. On the average, we feel that we are not average. Most of us feel that we are a cut above average. We do not admit to feeling stressed out or anxious about the future.

Our Primary Goals

But what do we want out of life? Barna's surveys suggest that we have four primary goals. These goals are all related to "being happy."

We want to be loved. We are driven to find acceptance from others, to belong to a group larger than what we ourselves represent.

Significant relationships are critical to our sense of self-esteem, and of purpose.

We want to make a difference. As young adults, this involves being socially sensitive so we may capture the attention of those in positions of authority and prove to them that we are significant. As we grow older, we want to do things that have a lasting impact. This is not to impress others but to support our feelings of self-importance and show that we can control our environment and direct the fortunes of others.

We desire security. The basic issue here is the elimination of fear. The way life is, we have a good number of fears about what may happen to us, so we strive to remove fear from our path.

We seek comfort. In America this usually means the acquisition of wealth and an abundance of leisure time. Comfort is both a sign of success and the experience of pleasure.

There are several ways to react or respond to this tension in our lives. We can deny it by ignoring the whispers of longing deep in our hearts and, like the wistful dieter who ogles rich desserts, say, "Oh no, I couldn't eat another bite; I'm so full already; no dessert for me."

We can react by fighting against the unfairness and emptiness of life. We can demand our rights, claim what's coming to us, and fight to get what we deserve.

Or we can respond by giving in to our fears and hiding from the pain. Alcohol, work, church, pills, and sexual affairs all promise to cover us with a temporary relief from the emptiness of unfulfilled longings.

The good news is that we are not stuck with these as our only options. Jesus said, "These things I have spoken to you, that my joy may be in you, and that your joy may be full" (John

15:11). The abundant life that Jesus offers to us is full and over-flowing. It must be ours, or our faith is a fraud! If there is no real joy and no abundant life, or if following Christ leaves us ultimately empty, unsatisfied, and restless, then Christ's death on the cross is a disappointing failure. It leaves us no better off than we were without him.

How then can we know the joy and fullness of life abundant? How can we know the power of God unleashed in our day-to-day lives? The answer lies in the restless pursuit of grace. It is not that we restlessly pursue grace, but that God in his grace pursues us.

Like so many characters in the Bible, our lives are filled with strenuous efforts to earn attention, make something happen, and help God fulfill his promises. In fact, we do everything humanly possible to avoid accepting the free gift of grace.

Adam and Eve were not content being merely the creation of God. They wanted to *be* God.

Cain wanted God's attention and acceptance on his own terms, and he murdered his brother when his disobedience was unveiled.

Abraham didn't believe that God would fulfill his promise of a child for him and his wife, Sarah, so he fathered an illegitimate son to try and fulfill God's promise through human efforts.

Moses couldn't wait to see the deliverance of his people, so he murdered a man and was exiled for many years.

King David was restless and unsatisfied, so he committed adultery and murder to gain the love and attention he thought he deserved.

The prophet Elijah felt afraid and depressed and wanted to commit suicide to ease the pain he was experiencing.

Judas couldn't understand why Jesus wasn't performing up to his expectations, so he betrayed him to his death, perhaps hoping that this would force the Lord to establish his kingdom on earth.

The history of humanity is a history of everyday people who take matters into their own hands. They are afraid to trust God. They refuse to step out in faith into the uncharted waters of tomorrow. They are desperately willing to do anything or try anything—anything but receive the grace that restlessly pursues us.

Grace turns our world upside down. It is so radical that it dims the shine on our trophies of success and achievement. It also heals the bruises and scars of our defeats and our trophies of failure. Grace reminds us that our greatest spiritual ecstasies, our peak moments, are not the measure of maturity, nor are our most painful secrets the measure of our character.

Paul, in writing to the Christians in Corinth, used himself as the example. He understood that the outer circumstances and standards by which we have learned to judge one another are no longer valid when we come face-to-face with God's grace. "Whatever any one dares to boast of, I also dare to boast of that. Are they Hebrews? So am I. Are they Israelites? So am I. Are they descendants of Abraham? So am I. Are they servants of Christ? I am a better one" (2 Cor. 11:21–23).

He also knew that pain, suffering, and disappointment would never make him a failure or separate him from the love of God in Jesus Christ. "Five times I have received at the hands of the Jews the forty lashes less one. Three times I have been beaten with rods; once I was stoned. Three times I have been shipwrecked; a night and a day I have been adrift at sea; on frequent journeys in danger from rivers, danger from robbers, danger from my own people, danger from Gentiles, danger in the city, danger in the wilderness, danger at sea, danger from false brethren, in toil and hardship, through many a sleepless night, in hunger and thirst, often without food, in cold and exposure. And apart from other things there is the daily pressure upon me of my anxiety for all the churches" (2 Cor. 11:24–28).

In spite of these hardships, Paul knew spiritual ecstasy. Visions, revelations, and spiritual experiences that on a human level might have been used to demonstrate his spiritual power. But he chose not to leverage himself spiritually. Instead he reminded them of a nagging problem that continually tormented him. "A thorn was given me in the flesh, to harass me, to keep me from being too elated" (2 Cor. 12:7). What's the point? Tremendous highs and dragging lows are both irrelevant. The highs don't last forever, but neither do the lows. If we focus on our personal experience, there will never be enough good, nor will we totally eliminate the bad to achieve a happy life.

We need a radical infusion of grace. Grace turning our world upside down. Grace setting us free from the inside out. Grace demonstrating over and over again, "When I am weak, then I am strong."

It is ironic that the things George Barna says we long for (love and acceptance, recognition and affirmation, security, freedom from fear, and personal comfort) can never be fully known on our own terms. We won't be loved enough, recognized enough, safe enough, or comfortable enough . . . until we allow God's grace to overwhelm us. St. Augustine said, "Our hearts will never rest, until they rest in God."

Paul said he prayed three times for his painful infirmity to leave him, but God answered him, "My grace is sufficient for you. For my power is made perfect in weakness" (2 Cor. 12:9). When we give up trying to make it happen on our own power and allow God's love to cover all of our lives, we discover this radical truth of the gospel: His grace *is* sufficient for us. His grace is enough when we stumble and fall. When we soar beyond our wildest dreams, when we have more than our share, and even when life is not fair, his grace is enough for us.

Enough is enough when in all of our lives we allow God to speak his comfort, assurance, and grace. Remember the very last words of Scripture: "The grace of the Lord Jesus be with you all. Amen" (Rev. 22:21, paraphrase).